Deciding What to

TEACH&TEST

THIRD EDITION

Fenwick W. English

THIRD
EDITION

Deciding What to
TEACH&TEST

Developing, Aligning, and Leading the Curriculum

CORWIN
A SAGE Company

For information:

Corwin
A SAGE Company
2455 Teller Road
Thousand Oaks, California 91320
(800) 233-9936
Fax: (800) 417-2466
www.corwinpress.com

SAGE Ltd.
1 Oliver's Yard
55 City Road
London EC1Y 1SP
United Kingdom

SAGE Pvt. Ltd.
B 1/I 1 Mohan Cooperative
  Industrial Area
Mathura Road,
New Delhi 110 044
India

SAGE Asia-Pacific Pte. Ltd.
33 Pekin Street #02-01
Far East Square
Singapore 048763

Printed in the United States of America

Library of Congress Cataloging-in-Publication Data

English, Fenwick W.
Deciding what to teach and test : developing, aligning, and leading the curriculum/ Fenwick W. English. — 3rd ed.
    p. cm.
Includes bibliographical references and index.
ISBN 978-1-4129-6013-7 (pbk.)
    1. Curriculum planning—United States. 2. Educational tests and measurements—United States. I. Title.

LB2806.15.E54 2010
375.001—dc22   2010009467

This book is printed on acid-free paper.

10   11   12   13   14   10   9   8   7   6   5   4   3   2   1

Acquisitions Editor:	Hudson Perigo
Associate Editor:	Joanna Coelho
Editorial Assistant:	Allison Scott
Production Editor:	Veronica Stapleton
Copy Editor:	Jeannette K. McCoy
Typesetter:	C&M Digitals (P) Ltd.
Proofreader:	Jennifer Gritt
Indexer:	Sheila Bodell
Cover Designer:	Rose Storey

Contents

Preface

America's Continuing Educational Canterbury Tales

The actors, voices, and travelers on the road to an improved public educational system in America continue to multiply and grow louder. It can be likened to a pilgrimage to a desired shrine at some far off juncture, a promised state where the schools are uplifted to a position of pure excellence from which individual prosperity and national security lie forever guaranteed and entombed. The reality, however, is that we are all pilgrims on the road to Canterbury, like Geoffrey Chaucer's late 1300s portraits of the stable of characters assembled at the Tabard Inn in Southwark going to the shrine of St. Thomas à Beckett.

The lives, stories, and motives of Chaucer's pilgrims comprise one of the world's literary masterpieces, and in it, Chaucer had perfected what is called "the rhyme royal," a seven-line stanza of poetry (*Concise Columbia Encyclopedia,* 1994, p. 164).

The rhetoric of the American pursuit to the shrine of national educational excellence is our political "rhyme royal," from the Reagan administration's proclamation of *A Nation at Risk* in 1983, the George W. Bush administration's *No Child Left Behind* in 2001, and now the Obama administration's *Race to the Top* in 2009. The fellow travelers in this pilgrimage represent a cast of characters from the most venal (pilgrims who want American education to wipe out global competitors in the international game of economic dominance) to the most pious and innocent (pilgrims who want to ensure that all children are eternally happy, proficient, and economically independent living in a world that is forever safe and just).

The assemblage of characters and interests in our national pilgrimage has seen the creation of an interlocking apparatus consisting of high ranking politicians in both parties, the issuance of national proclamations and reports, a wide range of state initiatives, independent manifestos from think tanks on the political left and right, independent foundation agendas and projects, and a volatile mixture of local political issues from bankrupt inner city school systems to battles to end school busing to attain the goals of integration regarded by some as an atavistic social remnant from the previous millennia.

The American educational shrine of public elementary and secondary education is wrapped in what Michael Parenti (1978) has called the *sacranda,* that is, its sacrosanct beliefs about its identity anchored in its core values. As Parenti (1978) observes, the *sacranda* represents, "The interests of an economically dominant class [which] never stand naked. They are enshrouded in the flag, fortified by the law, protected by the police, nurtured by the media, taught by the schools, and blessed by the church" (p. 84). The *sacranda* are the basic narratives Americans resonate to as they picture the good life, the desired social system, and the outcomes they want from the existence of a *political ladder* to improve one's lot in the economic system or simultaneously preserving one's place in that same system.

Therein represents one of the most fundamental tensions in American educational life. The pilgrims on the road to our educational shrine are going to worship because some of them see their journey as a way to advance their own interests and well-being, while others see it as a way to ensure their position of influence is retained. What Parenti (1978) tells us is that the shrine itself is a symbol of the dominance of those who hold the power because its definition of importance was determined by them. Bourdieu (1984) has called this intersection of interests, attitudes, values, and position in the social structure a *habitus* and comments that while there is *space* between those of higher and lower position, both classes work within the same structure. It is, therefore, *homologous*. As in the road to Canterbury, the journey to the shrine is the homologous rationale and structure that encompasses a wide range of interests, motives, and visions for the pilgrims travelling within and on it.

This book, therefore, fits into the American pursuit of a more perfectible public school system. First released in 1992 by Corwin Press, it has enjoyed a robust and extended period of attention and sales. That in itself is testimony that readers found something in its exposition and explanation worthwhile and useful. But the book is more than a technical and temporary solution to the issues that continue to fuel the national debate about educational excellence. At a more profound level, it raises questions about our beliefs, goals, and aspirations and whether any political agenda, no matter how noble and wrapped in its most potent symbolic *sacranda,* is anything more than the difference between the stories of the pilgrims and their collective ride toward a secular shrine and their own revelations, shortcomings, compromises, and contradictions. Perfectibility is always a journey. Perfection is a shrine. This work is about the journey, and as such, it will include some revelations, inevitable shortcomings and compromises, as well as its share of contradictions. We are all travelers on the same road, and this book is simply my story in our continuing educational *Canterbury Tales.*

Acknowledgments

Corwin wishes to acknowledge the following peer reviewers for their editorial insight and guidance.

Elaine Edmonds
Adjunct Professor
Metroplex Graduate Cohort Program
Concordia University Texas
Austin, TX

J. Jeannette Lovern
Associate Professor, Curriculum and Instruction
College of Education
Eastern Kentucky University
Richmond, KY

Salvatore F. Luzio, Sr.
Adjunct Professor of Graduate Education, Wilkes University
Undergraduate Adjunct Professor of Teacher Education, Keystone College
Wilkes-Barre, PA

Jane McDonald
Education Consultant in Leadership Development, Team Building, and Curriculum Development
Recipient of George Mason University Teaching Excellence Award
Reston, VA

Marilyn Meell
Director of Offsite Instruction
School of Education
Concordia University, Ann Arbor
Ann Arbor, MI

About the Author

 **Fenwick W. English** (PhD, Arizona State University) is the R. Wendell Eaves Distinguished Professor of Educational Leadership at the University of North Carolina at Chapel Hill. Formerly, he served as a program coordinator, department chair, dean, and vice-chancellor of academic affairs at universities in Ohio and Indiana. As a K–12 practitioner, he has been a superintendent of schools in New York, an assistant superintendent of schools in Florida, and a middle school principal in California. He also had a stint as an associate executive director of the American Association of School Administrators and a partner in Peat, Marwick, Main, & Co. (now KPMG Peat Marwick), where he was national practice director for elementary and secondary education in Washington, DC. He recently served as editor of the SAGE *Handbook of Educational Leadership* (2005) and the SAGE general editor of the *Encyclopedia of Educational Leadership and Administration* (2006). His most recent books are *The Art of Educational Leadership* (2008), released by SAGE; *Anatomy of Professional Practice* (2008), released by Rowman and Littlefield; and *Restoring Human Agency to Educational Administration* (2010), released by Proactive Publications of Lancaster, Pennsylvania. He served as a member of the Executive Committee of the University Council of Educational Administration for seven years and was President in 2006–07. Currently, he is a member of the National Council of Professors of Educational Administration Executive Board. Dr. English has served as a curriculum consultant and/or lead curriculum auditor to some of the nation's largest school systems.

Among the recent school systems where he served are the Fort Worth Independent School District, Texas, the San Antonio Independent School District, Texas, the Baltimore County Public Schools, Maryland, the Wake County Public Schools in Raleigh, North Carolina, and the Anchorage Public Schools of Alaska.

Introduction to the Third Edition

There is an air of desperation about curriculum and testing decisions in the schools today. That tone and the accompanying drama they produce have been the result of the publication of test scores and the inevitable comparisons they bring in the public mind. Tests are bestowed with a neutrality, perfectibility, and finality that belie their development and use in real life. They are debated and discussed in legislative halls and editorial pages without any knowledge of the motivations, assumptions, false hopes, and flaws that were part of their creation and continue to be present in their utilization. Where once tests were *means to ends,* they have now become ends in themselves. To some, it doesn't matter what they measure or if they measure anything significant at all; it only matters that they be high. Whereas *learning* used to be the purpose of education, now it is scoring well on tests no matter what they are. Today, schools are considered "good places" not because of their environments for learning and the development of human growth across the board on measures of becoming more fully human and humane, instead they are judged according to their confinement to the "core" academic subjects—not defined as the Greeks did, which included music and physical education, but as the Puritans did in their quest to eliminate sin. Testing used to be a service to the main function of education. Today, it is a business with a definitive bottom line squarely set in a "for-profit" market model.

What is lost in the testing discussion is that it is part of the larger social struggle for power in our society. Tests are not only a particular type of tool, but also they are weapons in that contestation. There are winners and losers with the employment of tests in the schools, not only within schools but also in the larger confrontations and movement in whole societies and between nations. The putative "Father of American Public Education," Horace Mann, found in tests a powerful weapon to advance his control of schooling. In Mann's classic battle with the Boston schoolmasters, he devised a test in secret, had copies printed, and then would take his horse and buggy to a local school, order the teachers to bring all students to the auditorium, and administer the test. After this scenario, he would drive away and later release the test scores with a blast at the ineffectiveness and inefficiency of the schools. He used this method to centralize state educational power. We are using the same method to propose decentralization and privatization today. In this scenario, tests are not diagnostic tools. They have become weapons in a test of wills. Schools whose pupil populations do not do well are assumed to be "poor," when the fact is that many are simply organizations serving the poor.

Most practicing educators know that many tests have little to do with any local, state, or national curricula. Any cursory "eyeball" analysis of such scores in the local media after the test results are released will inevitably show that the highest scores come from the richest areas of the state or city and the lowest from the poorest areas. The injustices meted out to poor, minority students in the name of tests are a national scandal. They are placed in double jeopardy—first because they are poor, and second because color is related to poverty. What can educators do when tests are used as weapons to punish someone for being poor, black, or Hispanic? The answer is to make sure students are prepared to take the tests. To do this well means to engage in *alignment* and to confront the cult of secrecy that surrounds many testing programs.

If a test is going to serve as a measure of accountability, there can be no secrecy. To be held accountable within the concept of *fairness and due process,* a person must know what is expected, have an opportunity to learn what is expected, and be provided an opportunity to demonstrate whether he or she can actually do the task. Keeping tests secretive violates due process. I've had this conversation with testing bureau personnel of many state departments of education, some of them quite heated. The logic embedded in accountability is not the same logic embedded in tests, particularly the norm-referenced standardized variety. Curiously, in private conversations, most of the representatives of the testing companies who sell the tests on the road agree with me. If they don't, they can't say so publicly. How can the schools do better on tests if they are kept secret? If the tests don't measure any specific curriculum, how can they be used to fairly assess any local or state curricula, the ones most teachers and administrators are really accountable to teach and supervise?

I find the naïveté of some of the testing advocates appalling. When a board of education threatens contractual nonrenewal of a superintendent who somehow can't improve test scores, the idea that one should not "teach to the test" is counterintuitive. The testing advocates want to believe that tests are neutral diagnostic tools designed to "help" schools become better. They ignore 30 years of research that shows that what drives most test scores has nothing to do with what is going on in schools or who is working in them but is predicated and anchored by the socioeconomic dispositions of school clientele. They want to continue to posture that knowledge is neutral and that the tests are assessing something open and equally accessible and available to all the students who are compelled to take them. They want to continue to believe that all children have an equal start to acquire the cultural capital that is included on test content, including the linguistic skills and conceptual fields in which schools transact their main business. Tests assume that there is a cultural and linguistic homogeneity present that is defied by anyone who is now working in schools that are becoming increasingly more diverse, especially in the nation's urban school centers. Schools still reflect and reproduce larger socioeconomic group divisions. They are Bourdieu's (1993) notion of *habitus* personified, and the testing industry reinforces such divisions by enshrining the same forms of cultural capital regnant in school curricula.

Deciding What to Teach and Test opened this conversation in 1992. It's still going on. I keep working in this vineyard only because of my outrage at the false cloak of impartiality that shields the testing business from the scrutiny it deserves. Tests do not treat all children with equality, let alone equity. The fact that the constant predictors of test performance are grounded in socioeconomic class, race, and gender reveal the deep and biased fault lines that permeate the larger society are reflected in the schools and reinforced by the industry.

We are not, as some of our politically conservative critics charge, the children of John Dewey. I wish it were so. We are, rather, the children of Frederick Winslow Taylor. The accountability movement is Taylorism personified, especially in the measurement of work, which testing represents in education. That it becomes fairer is the key to its continuation, though its recasting around more neutral forms of cultural capital is a much better solution, but one that would be stoutly resisted by the elites who now control the schools. Tests and the cultural capital they represent are not now fair, open, or equitable. They remain locked in the false scientism and genetic frauds of the 19th and early 20th centuries that, unfortunately, promise to be extended into the new century. That we should initiate the process of untangling this racist, sexist, and class-based system masquerading as meritocracy is long overdue.

Editor's Note: Fen English is one of the most insightful and creative educational scholars of our time. In this completely updated revision of his seminal work on improving student achievement he continues the journey by exploring current relationships between learning and mere scoring.

Most important, he expands the discourse with an exciting new chapter on curriculum leadership, including illustrations for the concept of organizational slack—as well as an expanded exploration of the importance of cultural capital in assessing the achievement gap.

CHAPTER ONE

The Function of Curriculum in Schools

School is about learning the values, norms, rituals, symbols, and designated knowledge of the dominant groups in power in any particular society. There are always many histories that exist in any given nation, and all of them are not always recognized or taught in the schools. So school learning is both written and unwritten. For example, schools teach an approved form of history, but they also teach students how to receive that history and what to think of it. Students may learn that in the naval bombardment of Fort McHenry in September of 1814 off Baltimore Harbor, Maryland, Francis Scott Key was aboard a British ship and observed the attack throughout the night. In the morning, the American flag was still flying over the fort, and when he was released, he wrote some verses that when put to an old English drinking song became the Star Spangled Banner. Over a hundred years later, the song was adopted by the U.S. Congress as the national anthem. This historical event could hardly be taught without a full range of values being involved, such as patriotism, allegiance, loyalty, reverence, awe, and pride, as well as an attitude that individuals that refuse to sing the national anthem are anti-American, despite the fact that such a refusal on religious grounds is also part of being an American and guaranteed in the U.S. Constitution.

The content of schooling in all of its forms (written and unwritten) is called the *curriculum*. This ancient Latin noun meant "a running, course" as in "conjiccere se in curriculum" or "a quick course at full speed, swiftly, hastily" (Andrews, 1854, p. 405). The importance of understanding the Latin roots of the concept of *curriculum* is that it was a *designed* experience. Someone or somebody had to give thought to the course to be run before the actual running, and just as importantly, it had to be run speedily. Because schooling represents only a portion of a human being's life, the curriculum is not the entire life but the designed life for the students in the school. The limitations of time itself comprise a kind of necessity to be "quick" about its use in schools.

There are different audiences for the curriculum in the schools: students, teachers, parents, taxpayers, accreditation agencies, government bureaus, other political bodies, and even society as a whole. The selection of the written content comprising the curriculum involves determining of all the things that could be included that are the most important. It is clear there is more to be taught than time is available (Rutter, Maughlan, Mortimore, Ouston, & Smith, 1979). The designation of the content of curriculum—whether that content consists of facts, figures, or in the terminology of Alfred North Whitehead (1959), "inert knowledge" that he claimed was "the central problem of all education" p. 7)—or the idea that knowledge should be learned in a problem solving active mode, or even that knowledge should be selected by the student and not the state, curriculum designation is a political decision and not a scientific one. The selection of the "stuff" that comprises curriculum content is about purposes and values, and it is about *power*.

Power is the catalyst that forges the selection of curriculum content in the schools. Somebody has to decide what is to be taught and ultimately what is to be learned. And since there is no scientific way to determine such things, the selection of the content involves framing an argument for what is most important to be learned in the brief time students have in schools. And since in the United States and most societies the public schools are agents of the state, and the state is run by those in power, the definition of the state, whether it is secular or sacred, becomes the screening framework for what is eventually included and excluded in school curriculum. Curriculum content is part and parcel of the political-socioeconomic system, especially in capitalistic countries, and its congruence to the values and perspectives of capitalism with an emphasis on the individual, competitiveness, and personal initiative become paramount cultural norms and form the cradle in which the curriculum is rocked (see Bowles & Gintis, 1976; Cole, 1988).

What is important to understand is that there is no "natural" curriculum in existence. School curriculum is a cultural artifact, and as an artifact, it is a socio-political-economic construct. It is neither good nor bad, right nor wrong, moral nor immoral unless such a discussion is anchored in a values perspective, or what Bourdieu (1984) has called "systems of dispositions" (p. 6).

One example of the politics of curriculum content is provided in the continuing protests in China and Korea over Japan's World War Two atrocities committed in their countries that were erased or soft-pedaled in Japanese school textbooks in 2005 (Lind, 2009). School curriculum represents the interests of the ruling class, and as Parenti (1978) observes, the ruling classes represent their interests and wrap them in the *sacranda,* which are the basic sacred symbols of a nation's identity. "The interests in an economically dominant class never stand naked. They are enshrouded in the flag, fortified by the law, protected by the police, nurtured by the media, taught by the schools, and blessed by the church" (p. 84). But Japan is not the only example of issues with a nation's *sacranda.* Lind (2009) reports that in France political rightests and socialists protested when President Jacques Chirac apologized for French participation in the Holocaust, which resulted in the expulsion of 75,000 Jews. Similar protests occurred in the United Kingdom when the archbishop of York proposed a national apology for the nation's participation in the slave trade or in the United States when a 1994 exhibit at the Smithsonian on the use of the atomic bomb in Hiroshima suggested it was unnecessary drew a U.S. Senate rebuke.

These examples show that a discussion about curriculum content involves the full range of values and perspectives that hinge on such questions as the nature of society and the kind of society a social system wants to become or remain. The nature of the educated person, the nature of the good life, the nature of human learning, and when capitalistic values become regnant, debate about cost and benefits and international global competitiveness—a perspective that sees a nation's fate connected to its share of a defined global market place with an abundance of material goods forming the core of its *quality of life* (see Horton, 2003; National Commission on Excellence in Education, 1983)—are also questioned.

What we know about human constructs is that they are never neutral; they fit into existing systems of power (see Bell, 1988; Bourdieu, 1998; Kerbo, 1983), and power is distributed unevenly in nearly every society in the world. Likewise, there is no such thing as "neutral knowledge." All knowledge is a source of leverage for those in power, and it is pursued to gain and to keep political advantage— a concept called "power-knowledge" by Foucault (1980). Debates about curriculum content are examples of politics and about whose values will prevail in a society where they can be disputed and con- tested (see Bates, 1993; Hirsch, 1988; Nash, Crabtree, & Dunn, 1997; Ravitch, 1974; Shor, 1986; Tyack & Hansot, 1990). For this reason Bourdieu and Passeron (2000) have called the power to impose mean- ings, as in the designation of curriculum content, as "the cultural arbi- trary" (p. 5); the authority to engage in that imposition, "pedagogic authority"; the development of curriculum for teachers to follow as "pedagogic work"; and the main function of institutionalized educa- tional systems is "to produce and reproduce the institutional condi- tions whose existence and persistence (self-reproduction of the system) . . . necessary . . . to the fulfillment . . . of reproducing a cul- tural arbitrary" (p. 54). In short, and despite political rhetoric to the contrary, the political function of curriculum is to reproduce the socioeconomic status quo. To do this, one must examine not only what the curriculum states and includes but also what it doesn't include and what remains silent.

It is against this montage of conflicting values and a continuing canvas of imposition and disposition that the topic of teaching and testing is discussed in this book. Former President Bush's education plan "No Child Left Behind" and President Obama's "Race to the Top" are simply examples of a failure to understand the full dimen- sions of the issues and problems of using the schools to confront socioeconomic inequities without recognizing the crucial role that teaching and testing play in perpetuating the very conditions they sought to ameliorate (see Ingersoll, 2003). It is also a form of what Mohawk (2000) has called "a revitalization movement" that is char- acterized as "generating a high level of enthusiasm around unrealis- tic expectations, often with tragic results" (p. 5).

Both of those plans and many that have come before seem to not recognize that the internal operations of schools and doing things better inside of them are (1) not culturally neutral practices no matter how much they embrace "best practices" because curriculum content itself is laced with ideologies in which they are defined and assessed, and (2) children from subcultures other than that approved by the elites who define the curriculum will always be at a disadvantage (see Solomon, 1992). Unfortunately, such children are often believed to be if not genetically inferior then culturally inferior.

For this reason the hinge of teaching and testing must always be examined closely and within the context of the times, or as Mohawk (2000) observed, "History is not simply a record waiting to be unpacked and examined but a series of emerging texts subject to revision and reinterpretation, each built on previous work" (p. 260).

1.1 WHAT IS CURRICULUM?

Among the many functions curriculum plays in the schools beyond a representation of the approved culture and perspectives adopted by the state and the groups that are in power within the state is that it is the sanctified content to be taught and as such, becomes the platform for subsequent testing. But as we shall see, testing does not isomorphically simply follow the designation of curriculum content. Often, tests have content of their own apart from what may be in the curriculum. So tests are never neutral tools, as the examples and content in them are loaded with forms of sanctified cultural capital. Bourdieu (1984) has noted that, "There is no way out of the game of culture" and what he reminds us is that the objectification of the approved and sanctioned culture embodied in curriculum and tests is that "the objectification is always bound to remain partial, and therefore, false so long as it fails to include the point of view from which it speaks and also fails to construct the game as a whole" (p.12). Even as this book speaks to teaching and testing, or testing and teaching, the perspective is not to assume that the content of either remains above serious questioning, nor does matching them in an effort to improve achievement on the tests relieve us of the responsibility of ultimately asking "who benefits from gains on these instruments?" The designation of curriculum content and the practices of increased testing as a form of measurement are more than the concern of educators or school boards. The Business Roundtable has been a powerful advocate for more testing in the schools. The interconnectedness of what Emery and Ohanian (2004) have identified as "an interlocking corporate-government-foundation-nonprofits network" (p. 59) show a tilt towards for-profit educational models and the privatization of public education, hardly a neutral political action agenda (see also Anderson & Pini, 2005).

When most school administrators think about "curriculum," they think about "curriculum guides." The word *curriculum* didn't come into widespread use in education until textbooks were used in preparing teachers in normal schools. That didn't occur until 1900 (Schubert, 1980). For a very long time, school textbooks took the place of curriculum in the nation's public schools. It was textbooks that established the content to be taught and delineated the methods used to teach them as well. To a very large extent, the domination of the textbook in curricular affairs continues into current times (see Fitzgerald, 1979; Nietz, 1966; Price-Baugh, 1997; Svobodny, 1987). The use of textbooks has been a standardizing effort to impose order on curricular anarchy over a long period of time (see Perkinson, 1985, p. x).

There are many different definitions of curriculum. Parkay, Hass, and Anctil (2010) identify at least five. Three of those definitions revolve around a designation of content, one regarding outcomes, and one includes virtually all of the experiences a student might have in school (p. 2). The focus of this book is about the linkage between teaching and testing, and while it is acknowledged that there are many unplanned occasions a student may encounter in school, unless they are anticipated, there is not much school personnel can do about improving test performance. Planning and anticipating what is to be taught and/or learned is central to controlling as much of the variance that may be the cause of poor or disappointing test performance as possible. Control is central to accountability. Most notions of accountability, especially those embodied in legislation that are punitive or remunerative, assume that school personnel are *in control* or *can control* those factors that will lead to improved test performance. For this reason, the definition of curriculum is that it consists of any document or plan that exists in a school or school system that defines the work of teachers, at least to the extent of identifying the content to be taught children and the possible methods to be used in the process.

Most schools have a variety of such *work plans* in place or available for teachers to use. Such materials may be textbooks, curriculum guides, scope and sequence charts, computer programs, accreditation guidelines, state department of education or state board guidelines, local board policies, or their specifications. All of these "plans" compete for the attention and loyalty of the classroom teacher. In many cases, these documents do not "match" one another, may contain contradictory advice or information, or may be so open to interpretation that contradiction arises when they are implemented. The definition of curriculum is that it is a document of some kind, and its purpose is to *focus* teaching within some sort of common boundary and *connect* the work of classroom teachers across boundaries because learning occurs across many years (English, 1987). By boundary is meant a grade level (as most schools are graded) within or across grades or within or across schools. Teaching in schools is too complicated to have teachers deciding at the last minute what to teach or just abandoning any systematic effort to think in advance about what they will be teaching on a day-to-day basis. The reality is that a variety of documents *compete* for the attention and loyalty of teachers to become the content that is actually taught, not the least of which may be the teacher as the sole determiner employing an eclectic mixture of sources and materials. Teachers remain at least semi-autonomous providers within schools and such autonomy, while at times a great barrier to the implementation of very flawed curriculum (see Freire, 2005; Giroux, 1988), is at other times a blockage to the kind of systematic, consistent instruction necessary to improve assessed learning on tests. The resistance of teachers to tightening the linkage between curriculum and testing is well known for a variety of reasons, not the least of which is the issue of the autonomy of the teacher to make such determinations as a professional provider according to his or her own judgment and the ability to downplay or negate the intrusion of testing in the life of the classroom (see Bidwell, 1965). Pay for performance schemes advanced by the Obama administration are a direct challenge to this long-standing recognition (Viadero, 2009).

1.2 CURRICULUM DESIGN AND DELIVERY

Curriculum *design* refers to the physical act of creating the curriculum for use in the schools. This may involve the purchase of textbooks (one kind of work plan and curriculum) and/or the writing of curriculum guides (another kind of work plan), and neither may be well connected to the other. This presents a real problem in considering the *alignment of curriculum* to the tests in use. School officials like to believe that teachers follow curriculum guides when in fact the research reveals they are much more likely to be dependent upon the textbook as the actual day-to-day work plan or "real" curriculum (see Apple, 1988; Venezky, 1992).

Curriculum *delivery* refers to any act of implementing, supervising, monitoring, or using feedback to improve the curriculum once it has been created and put into place in schools.

1.3 CURRICULUM COORDINATION AND ARTICULATION

Common in the vocabulary of most curricularists working in schools are the concepts of curriculum coordination and curriculum articulation.

Curriculum coordination refers to the extent of the *focus* and *connectivity* present laterally within a school or a school district. For example, if one were to ask, "What do four teachers of U.S. History I have in common at high school 'X'?" This would pertain to the extent that there was some expected focus and connectivity between these four teachers and their classes in a common curricular area. For *curriculum coordination* to exist, the four teachers do not have to be doing exactly the same thing at exactly the same time. The extent of similarity—that is, focus and connectivity— would be expected to vary some as the teachers adapted the content to be taught to the differences in the learners in their classes (see Figure 1.1).

Curriculum articulation refers to the focus and vertical connectivity in a school or school system. For example, if one were to ask what the level of focus and connectivity were from those four teachers of U.S. History I to any class of U.S. History II, one would be questioning the extent of curriculum articulation present. It would be possible to secure a coordinated curriculum without necessarily dealing with issues of articulation. One could have all the teachers in one grade or subject focused and connected without dealing with the teachers at the next grade or level. The same problem can exist between schools within the same school district. Table 1.1 illustrates the commonality and difference between curriculum coordination and articulation.

Figure 1.1   Curriculum Focus and Connectivity Issues

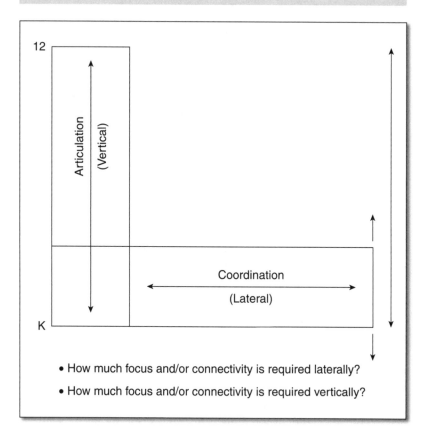

• How much focus and/or connectivity is required laterally?

• How much focus and/or connectivity is required vertically?

Table 1.1   Design and Delivery Issues Relating to Curriculum
Coordination and Articulation in Schools

Issues	*Coordination*	*Articulation*
Design issues	Define in the work plan the required levels of focus and connectivity desired to optimize student performance laterally.	Define in the work plan the required levels of focus and connectivity desired to optimize student performance vertically.
Delivery issues	Monitor program to ensure design integrity laterally.	Monitor program to ensure design integrity vertically.

1.4 COMBINING DESIGN AND DELIVERY ISSUES IN SCHOOLS

The several dimensions of dealing with curriculum in schools are shown in Table 1.1, which illustrates the possibilities and concerns of design and delivery issues relating to coordination and articulation in schools. On paper, these issues look reasonably simple. In the actual operations of schools and school districts, they become very complex.

Part of the problem in attaining design coordination and articulation is that teachers involved in curriculum construction may not agree on what the desired level of focus and connectivity should be. In part, this concern has been forced upon them by state or local testing programs that resolve these issues by testing students at a given level of focus and specificity. Then, as schools begin to engage in curriculum alignment with tests (a practice called "backloading"), the definition of the test focus and connectivity becomes that of the curriculum.

Of course, teachers are loath to define their work any more precisely than is necessary because to do so invites a concomitant type of supervision on the part of administrators and supervisors that changes the autonomy they currently enjoy and hence the *control* of their work (see Ingersoll, 2003; Lortie, 1975). Supervision involves monitoring the fidelity of the delivery of the curriculum compared with its design. This can occur even without interfering with the classroom teachers' usual prerogatives of deciding what kind of methods to use to teach with any given curriculum design.

At the root of this issue is the concept that once the curriculum content is adequately defined (a design issue), the teacher is obligated to teach it (a delivery issue) in some reasonably competent manner. Supervision involves an estimate of the adherence or fidelity of what is taught (not necessarily how it is taught) to what was supposed to be taught. This is the process of content design to content delivery.

Curriculum articulation is often lost within the structure of schools in which an egg-crate-type physical environment invites and encourages teacher individuality, isolation, and idiosyncratic responses. The issue is accentuated by school building to building autonomy and isolation involving authority within and across school sites (Bidwell, 1965).

Many a nice curriculum design, which was designed to enhance focus and connectivity within and across school sites, disappears in the reality of the chasms and gaps in the respective spheres of teacher and administrative autonomy that exist within school districts. This is why school organization has been labeled "loosely coupled" (Weick, 1978).

This organizational "fact of life" is perhaps the greatest barrier to the improvement of test performance because all testing scenarios implicitly assume that some focus and connectivity are present in the school system, otherwise, all commonality would be lost, and with it the basis for the comparison of individuals and groups assessed.

The presence of a minimum of commonality is a requirement for a test to provide important information about what is going on in school systems. What tests usually explain is *what isn't going on* in schools and school districts, which is why socioeconomic level remains the single largest predictor of pupil achievement as opposed to the actual curriculum in schools. The minute that curriculum becomes focused on and connected to, as well as aligned with tests, the influence of socioeconomic level on test performance begins to decline. This phenomenon is one of the most important correlates of the "effective schools" movement. These "effective school" procedures, once employed, decrease the predictability of socioeconomic determinism from test performance, which means poor kids can do better on tests if they are taught properly and well. Whether or not the actual *achievement gap* can be erased remains to be seen because curriculum content is not neutral with regards to the cultural differences that exist across any given society (see Solomon, 1992; Solomon, Booker, & Goldhaber, 2009). Some preliminary evidence does indicate that the gap can be reduced (Moss-Mitchell, 1998).

1.5 FORMAL, INFORMAL, AND THE HIDDEN CURRICULUM

There are at least three different types of curriculum in schools. One is the *formal curriculum.* That is the one that usually appears in curriculum guides, state regulations, or officially sanctioned scope and sequence charts. This is the one that is debated in public.

The second type of curriculum is the *informal curriculum*. This curriculum represents the unrecognized and unofficial aspects of designing or delivering the curriculum. For example, in *design,* the informal curriculum would represent the "values" at work in selecting curriculum content that is only tangentially "public." Such a value base is always at work when it comes to selecting the content to be included in schools.

The informal curriculum may be the one in *delivery* that is epitomized in various "tracking plans" that group children by ability and then differentiate among them by delivering a very different curriculum. The informal curriculum also involves the subtle but important personality variables of the teacher and the way these interact with students positively or negatively to encourage improved pupil learning.

The informal curriculum also includes learning how to take tests and coming to understand what tests mean to engaging in judgments about students and their potential success in schools. The student becomes increasingly aware that the judgment made about him or her by a teacher represents one that is total and often *socially deterministic.* Many come to accept the teacher's definition of their potential as that of society. If the students represent a group at odds with the more dominant group in society that teachers represent, they may come to feel of "less value" as persons (see Bernstein, 1990, p. 171).

Then there is a *hidden curriculum.* This curriculum is the one rarely discussed in schools. It is not even recognized by many educators who work in them. The hidden curriculum is the one that is taught without formal recognition. For example, American children are taught to be "neat and clean," "on time," and "respectful" to teachers. These "lessons" are rarely contained within formal curricula. But they are powerful conventions and norms that are at work in schools nonetheless.

The hidden curriculum contains "structured silences" (Aronowitz & Giroux, 1985) that embody expectations and presuppositions about social conduct that often place disadvantaged students "at risk" in schools and work against them by being ignorant of the inherent cultural biases that are embedded in school rules.

For example, a teacher of Native Americans complained about the lack of respect Indians seem to have for her because they would not look her in the eye. Indians were "shifty" and deceitful in her view, and this was an observable behavior that manifested this trait. This teacher was culturally unaware that in Indian life, *one does not look directly at* a person respected as being in authority, for to do so would be a sure sign of disrespect. This same characteristic is present in a variety of Asian cultures as well.

Other examples of the hidden curriculum that are distinctly cultural are learning the "correct" speaking distance in relationship to how loudly one talks and how closely one stands to another person in verbal discourse (see Hall, 1977). These "lessons" are all taught in school without being in any "curriculum guide" or textbook. Bourdieu (1977) has called this aspect of curriculum a *habitus*. A *habitus* is a "system of transposable dispositions," and it governs how one engages in "bodily comportment, say, to act or to hold oneself or to gesture in a certain way," and such bodily dispositions "encodes a certain cultural understanding" (see Taylor, 1999, p. 42). As children enter the school, many from different cultures who have learned how to comport themselves in a different *habitus* are immediately at odds with that embraced by the school in which the formal curriculum is structured. In this sense, a *habitus* represents the rules, and these "rules" undergird the development of curriculum, how we think about what is in and what is out of it. Bernstein (1990) has called these types of learning "tacit," meaning that their acquisition is part of the culture but not taught directly, and they form part of a coding system in use in schools that he has called "pedagogic grammars" (p. 3).

Too often, curriculum developers are not even aware of the *habitus* in which their work is founded. We shall return to this point later in a discussion of testing. There are three *other* curricula as well. They are the *written curriculum,* the *taught curriculum,* and the *tested curriculum.* These three curricula deal with content and express the absolute possibility that there could be in schools three unrelated "contents" floating around, unconnected to one another.

Table 1.2 illustrates a 3 × 3 curriculum matrix that contains all six dimensions previously discussed.

Most school administrators only consider the formal written, taught, and tested curricula in their work. This book will attempt to integrate all these versions of the "curriculum" to help school administrators use the power of a fused approach in improving pupil learning in schools.

Table 1.2   The 3 × 3 Curriculum Matrix at Work in Schools

Curriculum	Formal	Informal	Hidden
Written	Curriculum guides Textbooks	Tracking plans	Lived rules
Taught	Content taught (Instruction)	Personality variables of the teacher	Authority role of the teacher
Tested	Standardized tests Teacher tests	Test behavior	Cultural norms Socioeconomic status

1.6 CURRICULUM AND THE *CULTURAL ARBITRARY*

Most curriculum developers in schools recognize that the selection of the content that is included in a curriculum is arbitrary because both culture and curriculum are human artifacts. There is nothing in the "natural world" that contains curriculum or the culture in which it is defined and then taught in the schools. The selection of curriculum content represents narrow choices among many. And those choices are embedded in sets of values. The same is true for the tests that assess the curriculum. While the tests may be "objective" in the sense that they are not biased in one way or another within the curriculum and/or test dyad, the actual content of both curriculum and test are very much indeed biased, that is, they represent a value-based choice that includes and excludes a great many potential subjects or perspectives that could be taught and/or tested in school classrooms.

The French sociologists Bourdieu and Passeron (2000) have called the adopted and sanctioned government approved curriculum "the cultural arbitrary." It is so designated because human culture and its premises and rules are socially constructed. As social constructions, they are then imposed on all the children in schools irrespective of their particular cultural *habitus.* In this near universal process, one *habitus* is selected and presumed to be the "best" of all possible choices for all children. That such a choice represents the combined political power of the state and of the elites that control the state is rarely thoroughly examined or even discussed. Every now and then, something surfaces that points to how school curriculum is mostly determined by power relationships. For example, in parts of South America, there is a resurgence of people speaking *Quechua* (pronounced *kichwa*), which is the language of the ancient Incas. Across parts of Peru, Bolivia, Argentina, Chile, and Ecuador, there are perhaps up to 13 million people who still use *Quechua*. This language was banned by Spanish colonial authorities after an Indian uprising in 1781. And even after this event, native peoples learned that to use *Quechua* was a sign of low social status, so when census takers inquired about which language was spoken, many native peoples would not admit their usage of it. Today, *Quechua* has come out from the cultural shadows with the election of the first *Quechua*-speaking President in Bolivia and the founding of the first *Quechan*-speaking university. The first television station for *Quechan* viewers has also been established near Quito (Simon, 2009). The emergence of the ancient language that is intimately connected to the Inca culture is a clear indication of how language and culture are linked to political power. First and foremost, curriculum content is defined and extended by the use of the power of the state. It is therefore very appropriate to label it as Bourdieu did (Bourdieu & Passeron, 2000) "the cultural arbitrary" (p. 16)

Bourdieu (1977) also characterized the acquisition of the dominant curriculum content as a form of cultural capital, akin to fiduciary value, and because it was determined by political power, such acquisition represented a form of wealth (pp.183–184). The schools were one of the primary social institutions where such capital was acquired and by which those who excelled, as well as those who were left behind, internalized it (Bourdieu, 1977, pp. 63–64). Those who were not successful, or as successful as those who were, came to believe it was "their fault" in their failure and not the curriculum content or school routines that were to blame. So, even if those students who were least successful came to despise the institution that relegated them to a tertiary social place and space in the larger social-economic spheres, the system that held them in their place was not directly challenged. This struggle also represents a contested sociopolitical space in society. While it could be a location for social change for whole groups of people, it is rarely such a place. The exceptions are pointed to by the dominant elites as "proof" that it is not the system that is wrong but those of the individuals in it who "don't work hard enough" or otherwise lack other characteristics or values that hold them down. In short, the victim is blamed instead of the perpetuators. From this perspective, the so-called "achievement gap" will be a constant presence in schooling in that it is a consequence of the social sorting that schools perform in every society. Schools are the place where the winners and losers are identified.

The infrequent battles over public school curriculum almost always represent struggles for supremacy in the values arena and sometimes spill over into the courts such as (see Bates, 1993; Delfattore, 1992).

1.7 CONVENTIONAL PRACTICES AND COMPLAINTS ABOUT CURRICULUM

Conventional practices concerning curriculum include that it is "developed" or created by teachers to assist them in identifying commonalities to teach within local and state policies. School curriculum is supposed to be independent of textbook adoption so that in theory, the textbook does not come to replace curriculum but is instead a means of implementing it.

Conventional ideas about curriculum include that it is the epitome of local control of the "content" of teaching, is responsive to local demands and priorities, and optimizes the peculiar interests and strengths of the teaching staff. It is supposed to have been created by writing a philosophy first and then filtering goals and other priorities through a tripartite data base of social needs, knowledge requirements, and the tenets of learning psychology. This approach has been called the "Tyler Rationale" (Tyler, 1949).

A. Problem 1: Curriculum Clutter

There isn't a veteran teacher or administrator who hasn't at some point in his or her career come to the conclusion that there is simply "too much" in the curriculum to teach, and a whole lot of it doesn't seem to be related.

The U.S. public school curriculum is replete with fragmentation, "itsy-bitsy" desiderata that, taken together, represent a kind of "crazy quilt" of topics and subjects. Such a curriculum lacks coherence and focus. It is extremely difficult to set priorities because each "piece" has a priority all its own. Furthermore, each segment has vested political interests behind it to ensure it remains "in" the curriculum.

The lack of a "grand design" in the U.S. school is the result of the extreme decentralization of curriculum practice over a long period of time (see Kliebard, 1986). Curriculum is "developed" at the national level in the form of textbook publishing and test use, at the state level with state guidelines and tests, and at the local level with local board priorities mixed in with local teacher autonomy.

Weaving in and out of these three levels are various movements and "reform cycles" that bring in new ideas and "subjects" and when dead, leave a bit of residue in the overall curriculum quilt (see Tanner & Tanner, 1990). These movements are often antithetical to one another, which reinforces the tendency to fragment and segment them inside schools. It's the only way they can be "contained" and extended without inviting chaos.

The only way curriculum reformers can work in refocusing the U.S. curriculum is to step outside of it because there is no sense in searching for a rationale that is internal to it to serve as a philosophy or theoretical umbrella to bring it together.

Examples of this type of approach would be Mortimer Adler's (1982) *The Paideia Proposal* or William Bennett's (1988) *American Education: Making It Work.* The problem with using an external rationale is that the values that support it are often not revealed or even stated. For example, Adler's rationale would eliminate all vocational education from the curriculum because he believes that it does not represent something of "timeless" value that would provide a "liberal" education. Adler does not envision vocational education as "liberal," a view that in some cases contrasts with historical facts; Plato himself in *The Republic* described an ideal curriculum as one comprising academics, aesthetics, and athletics.

In Plato's curriculum, there are no electives or cocurricular subjects. All three constitute a tripod of a whole curriculum that was based on the idea that the development of a human being had to involve the mind, the body, and the soul. Plato's elementary school curriculum comprised music and gymnastics. The secondary curriculum was centered on the military. Only in higher education were the academics finally pursued (see Pounds, 1968, pp. 40–41).

The lack of a coherent, rational approach to the conception of curriculum in U.S. education is foremost political; second, economic; and third, educational. The political divisions of federalism and the lack of a central ministry of education have meant that neither the government nor its political agents and agencies could define or enforce anybody's curriculum as overt policy. The economic issues relate to class and race divisions interspersed with socioeconomic position. Poor people historically have had very few options to select their schools or their curriculum.

Finally, as an educational issue, the education profession itself has been unable to come to terms with what ought to be taught or learned in U.S. schools for any length of time. The void has largely been filled by the textbook publishers.

The solution to curriculum clutter is to engage in the development of an overall rationale or philosophy that helps develop the boundaries to examine the age-old question, "What is worth putting in a school's curriculum?" This issue will be dealt with in Chapter 2.

B. Problem 2: The Influence of Testing

The phenomenon of testing has continued to expand in recent times. Indeed, the testing industry is a billion dollar a year business in the United States with an estimate that between 114 and 320 million tests are administered each year (Madaus & Kellaghan, 1992, p. 126). As the individual states have adopted various types of statewide measures and the scores on these instruments are made public, the impact of testing has become more pervasive in identifying what is of most worth to teach or learn. The answer has become, almost by default in the absence of any larger rationale, *whatever the test is assessing.* So tests and test makers have come to occupy a primary role in defining curriculum content because it is quite natural to want to do "well" on the tests by making sure students have been taught what they need to know on them.

Thus "teaching to the test" is not only logical but also impossible not to do because it is the test that has come to sanctify the nature of "successful teaching" and "successful schools." Pedagogically, there is nothing wrong with teaching to the test as long as it does not mean cheating, that is, giving the students the correct answers ahead of time in some unethical way so that inferences about the learning the tests measures are compromised. But such practices have to be contextually situated in much larger issues that usually involve measurement, validity, and the base from which a whole range of political issues must be resolved. The phrase "teaching to the test" is widely misunderstood by the public and many professionals who work in the schools. We shall try and deconstruct it in this book.

C. Problem 3: Site-Based Management and Decentralization of Curriculum Development

U.S. education has swung from localized centralization to decentralization and back over a long time period (see Kliebard, 1985). We are just now emerging from a long period of immersion when site-based management was enshrined as the "one best way" to administer educational programs. What we have discovered is that when testing is centralized in top-down state managed accountability systems, it makes little sense to site-base a curricular response and risk the loss of alignment, and that includes textbook adoption and the use of other instructional resources.

If curriculum development is site based, then testing should also be site based because in that manner schools can be held accountable for the "match" between the two. If this is not the case, then curriculum development creates content not a part of any testing scenario. Test scores may decline due to lost alignment.

To improve pupil test performance, it is necessary to improve the match between curriculum content and test content. This means "tightening" the relationship between what becomes the written curriculum, the taught curriculum, and its "alignment" to the tested curricula.

That relationship has been called "quality control" (English, 1978). It is shown in Figure 1.2.

Quality control means that with specific actions, a target or goal (the written curriculum) becomes the basis for defining the work to be done (teaching), and both of these in turn are part of (aligned to) the tested curriculum. An administrator can "tighten" in any one of three ways. But "tightening" does not work unless all three are correlated (aligned).

Site-based management is a workable solution as a way to optimize the selection of methods or means at the local school level to optimize the "match" in quality control because it is at this level where "teaching" is actually delivered.

Figure 1.2   Quality Control in Curriculum Development

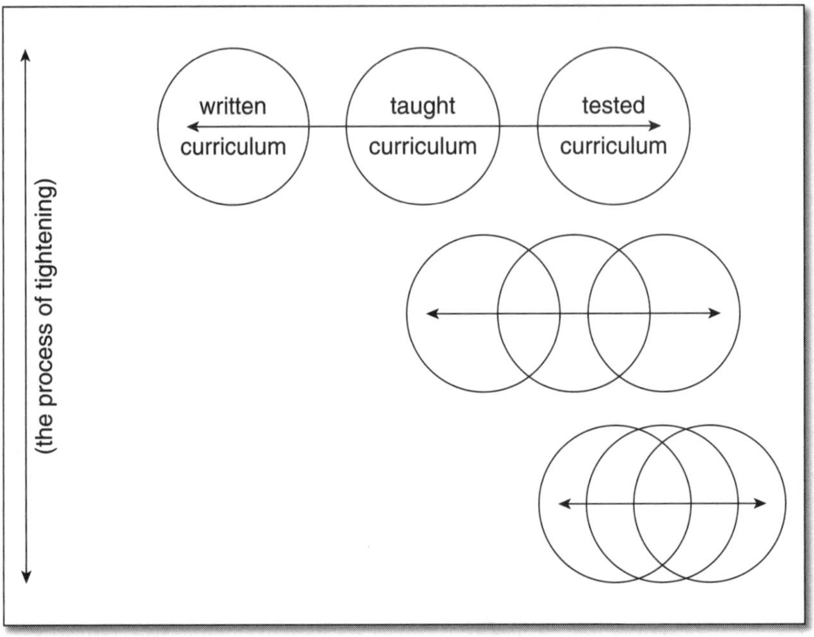

D. Problem 4: Loosely Coupled Systems and Teacher Isolation

Educational systems and the schools within them are not tightly interconnected. There is a great deal of "slack" between individual schools and the larger school system (English, 2008). Many contemporary critics propose cutting the individual schools "loose" from the system itself for all but the most perfunctory of duties (Maxcy, 1991). Whether or not this strategy is successful in improving pupil achievement, however, is in part a function of how success is measured.

If tests are used that presuppose a cumulative curriculum taught systematically over the years and across school buildings, then site-based management will not improve scores on these instruments because the "cumulative" impact of focused teaching is jeopardized. If each school becomes a school district, curricula sequence is often sacrificed. What is gained as a short-term benefit from being "liberated" from a highly bureaucratic and centralized system is lost as test scores fall.

Even if one takes steps to tighten the relationships between schools (curriculum articulation), the simple fact that schools in most school districts now are only minimally related one to the other presents barriers of geographic and physical dimensions of considerable magnitude. Much tradition has to be overcome in improving the correlation between the written, taught, and tested curricula due to the tradition of "loosely coupling."

The major avenue open to school districts regarding "tightening" (or quality control) is to tighten only in areas where it is required and not in every curricular area. These steps will be discussed in detail in Chapter 2.

We differentiate here between teacher autonomy and teacher isolation. There really is no way to observe teachers and adjust the curriculum in a direct one-on-one manner because teachers only have a small "piece" of the total curriculum, observation is always obtrusive and changes the classroom environment, and principals can't be present for a very long time given the excessive spans of control most must live with in the day-to-day operations of their schools.

For these reasons, modern supervision and monitoring depend to a large extent on getting teachers to monitor themselves and "training" teachers to follow the curricular materials published by the local or state agencies involved. The more difficult the testing scenario is, the more district officials may resort to the publication of materials that become more detailed and often more routinized.

Such practices may have the unhappy effect of "deskilling" teachers (Apple, 1979). The simple fact is that the more tests are used to calibrate the success of learning in schools (and by inference of teaching), the more curricular materials are developed to focus (and thus limit) the viable options teachers may select in curricular delivery. The use of any materials, however, ultimately has a similar impact.

The important question is this: Are the limitations consciously imposed after deliberate decision making, or are they imposed by system requirements? If the intervention is by system requirements, school districts have a special obligation to fully explore the hidden issues at work in the development of curricula that focus the work of teachers in classrooms. The real question is then, "Focusing by whom to obtain what for whom?" The heart of that question involves considering who the real clients of the schools are (children or society) and who is working for whom (teachers for administrators, for society, for children, or for themselves; see Courts, 1991). There is a difference between providing space for teachers to customize the curriculum and permitting teacher isolation that may compromise the strength of a curriculum to adequately prepare students for high-stakes testing.

E. Problem 5: The Deadening Impact of Textbooks

Textbooks are big business in education. In fact, it is estimated that "thirty percent of all books sold are purchased by the educational system, and the elementary school and high school market accounts for approximately 16% of total annual sales." (Keith, 1991, p. 45)

"The writing in most textbooks, particularly in the elementary textbooks, is choppy and stilted," notes Harriet Bernstein (1985, p. 464). She blames "states and cities that have mandated the use of readability formulas to determine the level of difficulty of a text." The use of such formulas makes the books harder rather than easier to read because it robs them of "connective tissue" that makes comprehension possible (see also Shannon, 1988).

Textbooks became a "fact of life" for U.S. schools after the Revolutionary War. Noah Webster sold his "spellers" from horseback and was perhaps the first to become wealthy from the sale of schoolbooks. His spellers were popular because they provided a curriculum to follow. U.S. schools in the nineteenth century were called a kind of organized anarchy, and the only thing that held them together was the textbooks used in them (Perkinson, 1985, p. x). But the domination of textbooks led to materials that appealed to the lowest common denominator among tastes and resulted in a "watered-down curriculum" and progressively easier and more bland content (Perkinson, 1985, p. xi).

The stranglehold of textbooks in U.S. schools continues. Goldstein (1978) has estimated that at least 75% of a pupil's classroom time involves the use of a textbook. These data suggest that the most important curriculum decision a district's officials may make is not which curriculum to "develop" but which textbooks to adopt. No other work plan in a school exercises the dominant and profound influence of school textbooks.

A large issue with textbooks is that they cannot just tell the truth and they cannot really teach children how to think critically. An example was the social textbooks of T. C. Columbia professor

Harold Rugg. At the height of its popularity, it is estimated that Rugg's books sold approximately 289,000 copies per year (Spring, 1991, p. 193). Because Rugg advocated that children learn how to "assume intelligent control of their institutions and environment," they came under attack from Hearst newspapers and from B.C. Forbes founder of *Forbes* magazine who tried to get the books banned from his own schools in New Jersey. Forbes believed Rugg's books were "viciously un-American" and they tried to convince "the oncoming generation that America's private-enterprise system is wholly inferior and nefarious" (Rugg, 1941, p.25). These attacks led to pressure from the Advertising Federation of America, the American Legion, and the Sons of the American Revolution that resulted in book burnings in school systems across the country and the Rugg books were reduced to annual sales of only 21,000 copies. Book publishers took note. Controversy ruins book sales. So much for the truth and so much for trying to help children learn critical thinking.

And the result of complaints and controversy also surrounds not only textbooks but the tests themselves. When test makers devise test questions, there are new guidelines about what is acceptable and what is not. According to Kronholz (2002), test item writers may not develop items which refer to marital status; grandmothers in rocking chairs; men as doctors women as nurses; teenage rebellion or hamburgers, birthday cakes, or sodas. Instead, there should be references to one-parent homes and grandmothers going jogging, occupations must be gender neutral, children must be obedient, and sodas are replaced with more healthful fruit juice and vegetables (p. B1). Ravitch (2004) has written a provocative book called *The Language Police* in which she avers that censorship by both the political right and left in curriculum, textbooks, and testing is unduly restricting what students can learn.

F. Problem 6: Simplistic Management Models

Unlike factories making standardized products that can impose rigid requirements for constructing machines where motions of production can be robotized for efficiency and precision, schools deal with a pliable humanity infinitely more complex and with a larger range of variance at every step of the process of education than the most demanding technical tasks that are known to exist in the rest of society. The human being is not only more elastic and variable than any other object to be processed, but he or she can also push back, resist, and reject the processes imposed. A human being is a restless and active coparticipant in education. The challenges of this situation are not understood well by policy makers, critics, and planners. They are almost always understood better by teachers and administrators who deal with the enormous psychic energy it takes to maintain a semblance of order and harmony in their classrooms and schools, even if they do not always understand the source of the tensions within their workplaces.

The elasticity of the human being to become interactive with a wide range of so-called "reforms" and defy them is due to the fact that reformers and policy makers assume a view that students and the schools they attend are static, that is, they can hold them constant while they manipulate the "changes" in them or on them. Groopman (2010) indicates that standardizing medical "best practices" made the same false assumption. What the policy designers and their legislative assistants took for granted was that patients would all respond the same to a putative "best practice." The reality is that in many cases, the success of the "treatment" is greatly dependent on an interaction with the patient and is therefore patient dependent as opposed to patient independent. Groopman (2010) summarizes the situation deftly when he says, "There is growing awareness among researchers, including advocates of quality measures, that past efforts to standardize and broadly mandate 'best practices' were scientifically misconceived" (p. 13). It is more than likely that many of the mandated school reforms that work in one place and not another are equally dependent in the same way. Students and schools are never static.

Another reason schools are difficult to change is that there is little energy left to change them as they are running because the tasks of maintenance are so "in your face" every moment of the day. Compulsory attendance in almost every activity means that there will always be tension and resistance. While learning can be conceptualized as "natural," schools are not "natural" places. They are deliberate social constructions with their own set of paradoxes and contradictions within them, and sociologists such as Bernstein (1996) have revealed the elaborate coding and classifications that mark them internally. Rhetorically, they may be there "to set people free," but they are "not free to do as they please" in them. Freedom pursued is not freedom lived. This paradox has been one of the constant criticisms of schools as being antidemocratic places and at odds with contemporary notions of governance and accountability (see Woods, 2005).

G. Problem 7: Cultural Capital and the Achievement Gap

There has been much hand-wringing and consternation about the achievement gap in American schools. In the United States, this has meant that certain racial groups consistently score below that of the dominant majority (see Tomsho, 2009). There are at least four explanations for this chronic underperformance phenomenon. They are biological, motivational, technical, and sociopolitical. All of them assume that the tests in use are not the causative agents themselves, that is, that they are neutral. This assumption must also be challenged despite evidence that the tests are not culturally neutral (English, 2002; Young, 2003), though much depends on how that neutrality or bias, as the case may be, is defined (see Jencks & Phillips, 1998). They are briefly presented here.

Explanation 1: The gap is biological, genetically established, and fixed.

This explanation has a long history in education and the schools. It can be traced to the ideas of genetic inheritance of Francis Galton (1822–1911). Galton wrote a book in 1869 titled *Hereditary Genius: An Inquiry Into Its Laws and Consequences* in which he studied men in various families in Britain who had attained recognized fame and social status.

He attributed their distinction to so-called "natural ability" and believed that it was general, that is, no matter what venue fame had been acquired, it was due to a general, inherited, and fixed element established at birth. White (2006) has criticized this idea of "natural ability" or what we would call "intelligence" today as lacking in evidentiary support and rooted in religious ideas of predestination in Lutheranism and Calvinism. This view believed that heaven was only for the select few and that entrance was established by birth. As White (2006) notes, "Some are predestined to salvation, the others to damnation. There is no middle ground. The saved, moreover, are few in number, and the many are damned" (p. 36). White (2006) also points out that those who make such claims must have some assurance that they are among those who can attain salvation. In a secular world, the answer was supplied by the notion that the IQ, inherited at birth and unchangeable, guaranteed that the writer was among those to be selected.

From this perspective the *achievement gap* is immediately explainable as the genetic difference between peoples and races in the world, and that trying to eliminate it is really folly. This is the view proffered by Hernstein and Murray (2004) in their book *The Bell Curve,* which accepted the view proffered by White (2006) that every person's role was predetermined at birth by a genetic code (see Conason, 2003, p. 138). The Hernstein and Murray (2004) book was excoriated as racist and elitist, ignored a huge part of the research evidence that linked school achievement to socioeconomic conditions, and used extensive literature funded by the Pioneer Fund that has sponsored and promoted white supremacist writings and authors and other racial eugenics perspectives over many years (Kincheloe & Steinberg, 1997, pp. 38–41; see also Kevles, 1999). And Murray has extensive and long-time connections to right wing think tanks such as the American Enterprise Institute (see Brock, 2004, pp. 47, 351).

If one actually believes in this perspective as Britain's Cyril Burt did, then the schools employ tracking to push the less bright (or the damned) out to their allotted stations in life. In a chilling summary of the trial of Nazi Adolf Eichmann after he was captured in Argentina and brought to trial in Israel, Hannah Arendt (2006) commented on the mass murder of the Jews by saying, "This sort of killing can be directed against any given group, that is, that the principle of selection is dependent only upon circumstantial factors. It is quite conceivable that in the automated economy of a not-too-distant future, men may be tempted to exterminate all those whose intelligence quotient is below a certain level" (pp. 288–289).

Explanation 2: The gap is due to leadership personality traits such as timidity, incompetence, and the lack of motivation (i.e., competition in the larger system).

The second explanation for the *achievement gap* is that the schools lack able leaders and are not run like businesses. This is the perspective proffered by writers such as the American Enterprise Institute's Frederick Hess (2004) and the Broad Foundation (2003). Those advancing this agenda see school boards, teacher unions, and schools of education as obstacles to be overcome or eliminated (see Gerstner, 2008; Riley, 2009). The motivation that unites them is a common agreement that schools need competition as incentives to become better, that educational leaders should employ the same procedures and models used in the "for profit" sectors of the economy, that educational leaders should be paid bonuses for improved test scores, and that teacher salaries ought to be linked to test score improvement. School superintendents don't need to be educators at all. They just need to be hard-nosed about attaining test score improvements. For this reason, the Broad people offer their own homegrown "training" program and sponsor their graduates with a variety of other incentives (Weinberg, 2003; Riley, 2009). Their superintendents have acquired the name of "gun slingers," and some openly show disdain for making a career in education (see Eisinger & Hula, 2008).).

The record of these non-educator superintendents shows some gains in system efficiencies and other cost-cutting measures, such as school closings and privatizing system services, but the record for significant and sustained student achievement gains is marginal at best. The fact that schools are not businesses and that the "for-profit" mindset that has dominated the private sector and led to severe excesses, scandal, and criminal behavior with prison time for business executives of some of the biggest corporations seems not to have been understood (see Cuban, 2004).

Explanation 3: Schools and school systems fail to adopt the kind of organizational and technical changes the situation requires.

This view of the *achievement gap* is that it is at least partially the result of the lack of rational and/or technical responses to specific organizational challenges. The principle challenge is that higher outcome responses, as embodied in such legislative mandates as Public Law 107–110 or *No Child Left Behind*, require tighter linkages within school systems than currently exist (English, 2008). This approach is the one that is supported by a large slice of the management literature of the last 40 years (see Thompson, 1967). It is the one that supports curriculum alignment as one of the major changes that will bring results, and there are data to support such assertions (see Downey, Steffy, Poston, & English, 2009; English & Steffy, 2005; Snipes, Doolittle, & Herlihy, 2002; Squires, 2005).

Explanation 4: Schools are controlled by the political elites who use them to reinforce their control of social order and their own position in it.

This view of the *achievement gap* is neither biological, personality defined, nor technical; it is rather political, economic, and social. The idea that the schools are the instruments of the reproduction of the existing social order is not new. Beginning with classical Marxism (see Bowles & Gintis, 1976) and the views proffered by Durkheim (1956) and Weber (Gerth & Mills, 1970) but more recently by Bourdieu and Passeron (2000), schools are seen as potentially transformative places where whole groups of people could be lifted from their social position to a different one, but whose role in the perpetuation of the social status quo goes largely unchallenged. Government programs designed to be transformative are shaped to "fit" into the status quo, and while they are superficially proffered by reformers to be of benefit to the more nonprivileged or marginalized groups, they rarely do so.

The research of Solomon, Booker, and Goldhaber (2009) offer some support for this claim. These researchers examined the effects of federally funded comprehensive school reform in Texas funded largely through Title 1 from the 1990s through the early 2000s. Comprehensive School Reforms funded a large number of external "reforms," including *Success for All,* and the *El Paso Collaborative for Academic Excellence* in 231 elementary schools. Only 16 schools created their own models for reform. When schools adopting comprehensive reforms were compared with similar noncomprehensive reforms, the researchers found no significant gains for the schools implementing reforms in reading but some for math. The gain in math was "slightly more than 2.5% of a standard deviation" (Solomon, Booker, & Goldhaber, 2009, p. 121). However, African American and Hispanic students "showed lower gains than this baseline group" and "at times negative gains" (p. 122). This research conclusion indicated that "only student background characteristics drive differences in student outcomes" (p. 119). The observation is consistent with Bourdieu's (1984) research on class distinctions and how they are reproduced in educational systems as well as that of Bernstein (1996).

In summary, the achievement gap is the result of many factors at work in school systems. The perspective offered in this book is that those that are controllable by educators should be employed in order to take the problem on *within* the existing set of socio-cultural-political constraints in which they exist. The controllable variables lie largely within the realm of rational and/or technical adjustments. The ultimate solution to the achievement gap dilemma that are due to cultural differences are much more difficult to tackle because they would involve approaching the mechanisms and role of the dominant cultural elites and their control of the content and nature of the school's curriculum. The nature of the resistance to this examination and possible change would be intense, in part due to the fact that culture itself is rarely perceived as a social construct but as "natural" in the eyes of those living within it. Those who do not adhere to the same cultural values are often viewed as "deviant" and are usually subject to censure, ridicule, rejection, or outright ostracism. This is not a struggle that educators are likely to win without a broader form of social consensus being developed for change. Until that happens, it is quite likely that those at odds with the cultural values and approved curriculum content in schools will be blamed for their "lack" of success in school, and much of their failure will not be seen as cultural difference but inherited, genetic capacity. This is the continuing tragedy of not recognizing the achievement gap as an artiface. Bernstein (1996) observed that the school unequally distributed knowledge, potentials, and its resources to students, and "It is highly likely that the students who do not receive these rights in the school come from social groups who do not receive these rights in society" (p. 8).

1.8 THE NECESSARY REQUIREMENTS OF AN IMPERFECT CURRICULUM

To be effective in schools, and especially in a relationship with high-stakes accountability tests, a curriculum must have at least three essential characteristics. As a work plan, a curriculum must provide for *consistency* (or coordination). It must provide for *continuity* (or articulation). A curriculum must also provide for *flexibility* in adaptation as teachers interact with students. *Flexibility* means that the curriculum must be open to some interpretations in terms of how and under what classroom circumstances the content is most optimally taught. This means that the curriculum must be capable of being changed by altering the sequencing and pacing of its delivery *without* fundamentally altering its design fidelity.

The reason is that with a work plan, the teacher is confronted with a range of differences in learners that eludes one of the most critical variables in planning any work activity, that is, *the absolute differences in the inputs* going into the work design itself.

From this perspective, the use of any manufacturing model in schools ultimately fails because nearly all operate on the assumption that somehow inputs can be *standardized.* With human beings, such an idea is absurd. Education cannot only not standardize people, but if education is effective, it leads to greater differences between students, not less. Thus, effective education quickly becomes destandardized in practice. Much of school ideology is aimed at "controlling" students by minimizing the differences between them, even as instruction is accentuating those same differences.

Effective school curriculum never attempts to standardize students but must, as a work plan, provide for focus and connectivity (coordination and articulation) *without* leading to mindless conformity where every teacher has exactly the same lesson on the same day from the same page in the same textbook. Such a situation would be profoundly unproductive and ineffective.

Curriculum in schools will always be in a state of tension between those requirements that are aimed at ensuring some sort of common content for all and those requirements that demand differences in approach, methods, and materials to attain the common outcomes. This phenomenon has been called "the paradox of administration" (Thompson, 1967, p. 150). It refers to a relationship known as "loose-tight" in organizational studies. When higher standards are imposed on a human organization, the usual response is to reduce slack, that is space between key functions. In schools, that would be the relationship between the written, taught, and tested curricula. This is true up to the point where in the delivery of the curriculum, the system must provide sufficient flexibility for the teacher to improvise and adapt the curriculum to the variance within the learner cadre. So the usual response of tightening functions and thereby loosening slack is effective only if it also simultaneously permits slack to exist in teaching that curriculum.

If common outcomes are required, the curriculum must enable teachers within schools to mix methods and materials very differently to come anywhere near close to ensuring the learning of those desired commonalities. Differences have to be allowed in order to consider what is an expectation for all. What that means for curriculum development is that, *as a process,* it must define the necessary levels of focus and connectivity without leading to standardization.

Human variability defies the use of manufacturing and/or production models in schools. Yet schools exist to create some sort of social consensus about the perpetuation of a common life mode for everyone. Schools cannot let everyone "do their own thing," or there would be no school. On the other hand, schools cannot force everyone to do the same thing without jeopardizing their function in a society that contains, sustains, and protects those very same differences among its peoples. That is the challenge that faces educators involved in designing and delivering curriculum in the nation's schools, now and in the foreseeable future.

Nowhere is this fact more apparent than in population projections for the United States and its racial and ethnic composition. It is now estimated that by 2050, whites will no longer be the majority. By that date, it is anticipated that the total U.S. population will be 399 million of which whites will comprise only 49.9%. While the black population will remain the same as it is today with 12.2%, Hispanics will comprise 28%, a gain of 13% from today. Asians will increase their presence to 6%, up from 4.4%. The point at which minority children become the majority is anticipated to be 2031 (Yen, 2009). With this projection in mind, it is clear that curriculum content will continue to evolve and become representative of larger social and cultural changes as the nation becomes more and more multicultural. The key point here is that the designation of what is the appropriate curriculum to be learned in the schools is not a scientific one but a political one. And in a democracy, politics is determined by a plebiscite. While educators may write the curriculum, the content of that curriculum is defined by the presence of much larger sociopolitical authorities. In short, we live in an imperfect world, and this will always be reflected in an imperfect curriculum. Any curriculum in a democracy where the content is determined by larger socioeconomic-cultural forces will necessarily contain paradoxes and contradictions. Only in a static society run by a ruthless and all powerful tyrant could the curriculum approach perfection. It would not be a world most of us would choose to inhabit.

1.9 A Clarifying Model of the Critical Curricular Relationships and Terms

Since the publication of the first edition of *Deciding What to Teach and Test* in 1992, there have been changes and modifications in curriculum practices nationwide. There have also been some essential confusions as well. Among the most prevalent obfuscation is the term *curriculum mapping*, which when I first used it in the 1980s (see English, 1980) referred to the *taught curriculum* and not the *written curriculum*. The idea was to find a conceptual way to indicate that the actual curriculum being delivered in the classroom could be quite different than the one put to paper by curriculum developers or designers external to the teaching process. The idea of discovering the actual curriculum in use as opposed to believing that one on paper was in use was to "map" that curriculum, the same as a surveyor would chart a new geographical territory by actually going there. I worked with many school systems in doing this kind of mapping and described it in some detail in English (1980), English and Steffy (1983), and English and Larson (1996).

Figure 1.3 shows this relationship as a clarifying model. To try and regain a foothold with the original use of *curriculum mapping*, I have resorted to showing the written, taught, and tested curriculum below by verb tense. The written curriculum is *the developed curriculum,* that is, the desired or intended curriculum to be taught in the schools. This is the future tense. The taught curriculum is the actual curriculum being delivered in the classroom, and the term for its content is a *curriculum map*. A curriculum map takes place in the present tense. I have also called this classroom content "the real curriculum" because it may be the only one students ever really know. It is also critical in assessment as the relationship between teaching and testing becomes the vital linkage via *curriculum alignment.* Finally, the assessed or tested curriculum occurs in the past tense, that is, it is representative of what the student has retained from the linkage between the future curriculum and the present curriculum, or the desired and actual curriculum designed and delivered. This important distinction has gotten lost in the confusion about *curriculum mapping* as advanced by Heidi Hayes Jacobs (1997) and others (see also Squires, 2005, p. 157) who never made such differentiations clear. In their approach, a curriculum map is the desired curriculum or the one teachers thought they might teach but not the

Figure 1.3   A Clarifying Model of Curricular Relationships and Terms

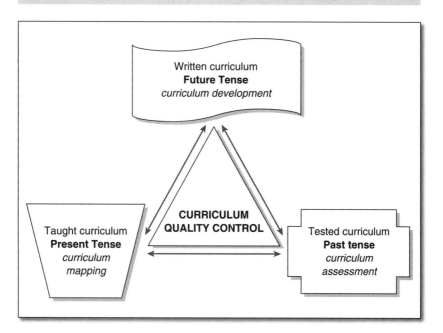

actual curriculum that was taught. Thus, it seems to me that the pretention of assuming that the desired curriculum becomes the actual curriculum is continued as before. This omission eliminates the important role of the classroom teacher in personalizing and individualizing the curriculum in its delivery. It is not sufficiently captured at all with the term *backward mapping*, which while perhaps defining what should be in the present tense is not actually what is being taught in the present tense.

CHAPTER TWO

A Template for Curriculum Construction

*C*urriculum development means that the school creates, adapts, or adopts various kinds of work plans for teachers to use to focus and connect their work in schools. As such, curriculum development includes the process of *textbook adoption* or the adoption of any other kind of document or material that exerts some shaping influence on what teachers choose to do in their classrooms.

When classroom teaching is influenced by these materials, it becomes *instruction*. Instruction is simply *systematized teaching,* which includes a single teacher but links all teachers together in some form of common purpose within a common curriculum core or content area (see Wallace, 1981).

The extent of commonality or connectedness is determined by the amount of "tightening" (or loosening as the case may be) required to bring together the written, taught, and tested curricula to attain desired learner outcomes. It all depends on the level in the organization where instructional or curricular variance (difference) is decreased or increased.

2.1 THE TRADITIONAL VIEW OF DEVELOPING CURRICULUM

The traditional view of developing curriculum in schools is shown in Figure 2.1. The process begins with something called *needs assessment*

39

Figure 2.1   Selecting Curriculum Content: The Traditional View

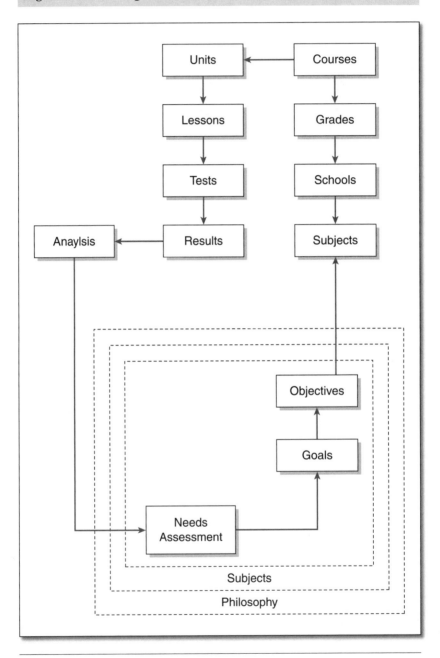

NOTE: This is an ideology: a closed system.

(Kaufman & English, 1979). From this, goals or targets are developed that must be broken down into smaller, more tangible, and measurable "chunks," called *objectives.*

Because most school curricula are organized around "subjects," the objectives have to be loaded into these clusters and located in schools, grouped into grades and courses, and within grades and courses further broken down into units and finally classroom lessons (see Ellis, Mackey, & Glenn, 1988, pp. 76–98).

Lessons are subject to tests of students, and from these measurements, results are obtained, reanalyzed, and fed back into the needs assessment cycle, which is repeated until test results and learner outcomes are identical. This is what is meant by "meeting the needs" of students in a certain interpretation of *needs assessment.*

A. The Ideology of the Curriculum Development Cycle

Curriculum development used to be considered to be a special kind of "engineering" (see Beauchamp, 1975). Today, it is generally recognized that curriculum development is very much a "value-laden" process that in no way resembles a neutral activity akin to engineering. Any kind of activity in schools must be judged not only by what its stated purposes may be (like developing curriculum) but also by what it is doing compared with the unstated purposes of schooling.

It is to the area of the unstated purposes of schooling that much criticism of curriculum development has been aimed in recent times (see McLaren, 1986). For example, if schools are conceptualized as places of opportunity for all children to climb the ladder to "the good life" in America, school curricula may be seen as liberating, with its focus on finding and honoring native abilities.

On the other hand, if schools are viewed as vicious sorting machines that are racially, culturally, and sexually biased places, reinforcing such biases in the larger society (Bourdieu & Passeron, 2000; Bowles & Gintis, 1976), then any curriculum that did not act contrary to these views would be also racially, culturally, and sexually biased.

A view of curriculum development that is insensitive to these larger issues is naive. The creation of work plans in schools reinforces *something.* To know what that "something" actually is requires a curriculum leader to look carefully at what is really going on in schools, not only at their stated purposes and public rhetoric but also at their hidden functions and unstated purposes. This is also a similar type of criticism regarding reform. If school reformers are not aware of the hidden functions of schools, they may not reform anything at all by making changes in them (Katz, 1987; Sarason, 1990).

Bourdieu (2008) has called the lack of awareness of those working socioculturally legitimizing places, such as schools, a form of misrecognition and observes that "thanks to a quasi theoretical reflection on their practice, conceals, even from their own eyes, the true nature of practical mastery; that it is *learned ignorance*" (p. 19).

B. The Myth of "Out There," Objective Knowledge to Serve as Curriculum Content in Schools

Figure 2.2 shows how most educators conceptualize the development of curriculum by creating a so-called philosophy. After constructing their "philosophy," they then select the knowledge that is consonant with that view. This approach is an example of "naive realism" (Lincoln & Guba, 1985, p. 37). The "naive realist" believes that there is only one "reality" that awaits discovery somewhere "out there." This outlook assumes there is only one interpretation possible of knowledge, and that it is "good" for all time and places,

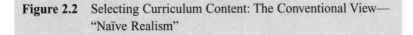

Figure 2.2   Selecting Curriculum Content: The Conventional View— "Naïve Realism"

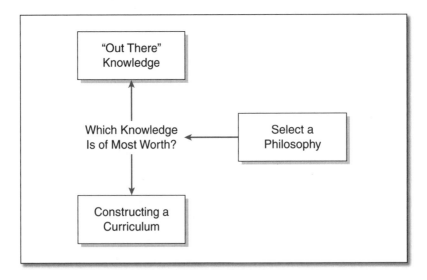

irrespective of historical context. The recurring controversy over "Afrocentric" curriculum is a good example of a conflict over interpretation of "facts." Afrocentrists want to replace Eurocentrists. The battle is over one "right" view as opposed to another "right view" when both views are probably possible.

The traditional curriculum development cycle is largely an exercise in ideology, that is, reinforcing a closed system of beliefs and answers without ever seriously questioning them. O'Neill (1981) has indicated that an ideology is different than a philosophy because it is anchored in social ethics, that is, notions of morality and politics, aimed at influencing social action and "are both a cause and an effect of fundamental social change" (p. 20).

The broken lines in Figure 2.1 represent these beliefs and answers as nonpublic and "hidden" values.

A needs assessment that functions within the unstated philosophy of school system operations and is centered in curriculum "subjects" is hardly an open-ended quest for truth. Instead, by being insensitive or oblivious to its own biases by not questioning them, it reinforces whatever they may be. A needs assessment cannot, therefore, be a truly open-ended search for values that may be selected by curriculum developers when some values are not stated or are "hidden" or are automatically selected a priori. This is why curriculum development traditionally conceptualized cannot be considered a "value-neutral" process like engineering.

The most common practice in developing curriculum is interested teachers being employed during a summer or after school hours to "write" curriculum. The teachers begin by identifying their "philosophy," which consists of listing their common "beliefs." Figure 2.2 is illustrative of this practice.

These statements may look something like the following:

"We believe all children can learn."

"We believe education should develop the whole child."

"We believe history should prepare students to live better in their world."

"We believe that critical thinking should be part of the curriculum."

Each of these statements is shrouded in values. For example, "We believe all children can learn," is a *tautology,* that is, true by definition. All children do learn in schools, though they may not learn what educators want them to or what is in the official curriculum. Human beings are learning all the time.

The statement "all children can learn" is akin to "all fish can swim." It reveals nothing and it predicts nothing. Yet it is commonly found throughout the literature of "effective schools" and appears in many schools' so-called philosophies (ideologies). A more accurate statement that would not be tautological might be this one: "All children can be successful in school."

The values embedded in the statement, "All children can be successful in school," are both overt and covert (hidden). The overt values are that, irrespective of background (socioeconomic level), race, or sex, it is believed that everyone can attain the indicators of achievement defined in the curriculum. No one is therefore excluded at the outset or excused from having to attain those outcomes. The overt value is egalitarian and encompassing. In practice, such a belief would challenge any procedure that "excused" some children from the same expectations indicated for "all children" for whatever reason.

At the same time, the *covert* values in the statement are that the "school," as it exists, is essentially correct for "all children" and that the burden is therefore on children to "adapt to" and "be successful" in them as *they exist*. Children therefore have to come to schools "ready" to learn in order to be successful in them. Parents have to ensure that their children are ready to learn. The "blame" for failure, therefore, rests squarely on the children and their parents and not on the schools if children don't learn in them.

That the school might not be "correct" is never considered in this context. If schools were to be accountable in this manner, the same statement might read, "All schools can be successful with all children," or "We believe that the school should be sufficiently flexible to be successful with all children." These statements would shift the locus of accountability from the students and their parents to the school and its staff.

Shifting the locus of accountability from the student to the school would make it more difficult for schools to behave in ways that have been clearly racist and sexist in enclaves in society. For example, a Texas superintendent once observed the following:

You have doubtless heard that ignorance is bliss; it seems that it is so when one has to transplant onions. . . . If a man has very much sense or education either, he is not going to stick to this type of work. So you see it is up to the white population to keep the Mexican on his knees in an onion patch or in new ground. This does not mix very well with education. (Montejano, 1987, p. 193)

If the schools as they exist are left untouched or unexamined in the development of curriculum, then whatever they do and for whatever reason, remains unchanged. Curriculum development that does not challenge what schools do and how they do it is not only naïve, but also it represents what Bourdieu (2008) has labeled an example of an "ideological apparatus" in which the school reproduces the established order and hides the perpetuation of domination in the process. Bourdieu (2008) comments, "The most successful ideological effects are those that have no need for words, and ask no more than complicitous silence" (p. 188). Too often curriculum development as traditionally conceived conceals such silences

The development of the "whole child" incorporates a view that the school must be concerned with what the learner is feeling, the level of inner aspiration present, and the complete fabric of living and perceiving things. Such a belief transcends the idea that the school is mainly a repository of knowledge and is concerned only with passing that knowledge along in some acceptable mode. The "whole child" idea can be interpreted positively or negatively, depending upon one's perspective on it. For some politically conservative parents, the "whole child" concept is an intrusion into the "privacy" of the home. For other parents, it represents a posture that they may see as positive and caring for the sensitivities and feelings of their children while they spend time in an institutional environment for a part of their day (see Purpel, 1988).

The belief statement, "We believe history should prepare students to live better in their world," puts a twist on the approach to dealing with the past. This statement would shape the past and provide meaning primarily from the value stance of the current time. Current meanings are always undergoing change. For example, Christopher Columbus was seen as a courageous and inspirational explorer in the past. To many, under the standards of the current time, he was a cruel, exploitative, racist colonizer who helped exterminate native Indian tribes via torture and intimidation. Whose interpretation is to be used to teach who Christopher Columbus was to American schoolchildren (see Mitchell & Weiler, 1991)?

The "critical thinking" goal is quite common as a curricular "belief" statement in schools. Yet most social scientists studying schools would deny that teachers or administrators really desire students to think critically at all. No school teaches children to criticize the Ten Commandments or the assumptions that support them. No school would create a curriculum that even hinted at the notion that monogamy would not be preferred over polygamy (though polygamy is an acceptable practice in other cultures). Students are not taught in schools to be critical of the work they may be asked to perform in factories and offices after they graduate from school and enter the world of work (see Simon, Dippo, & Schenke, 1991). In the words of anthropologist Edward Hall (1977, p. 205), "School life is an excellent preparation for understanding adult bureaucracies: it is designed less for learning than for teaching you who's boss and how bosses behave and keeping order."

Critical thinking usually narrowly refers to solving higher-order decontextualized mathematical problems, working in specified (but socially acceptable) art media, or working in one of the "hard" scientific disciplines like physics, chemistry, or in biology (sufficiently roped off to exclude dealing with the theory of evolution).

Critical thinking never means learning to be skeptical or truly critical of one's own cultural values and biases, the way the school is organized, what the teacher may choose to teach or the way he or she chooses to teach it, or school routines such as rigid adherence to schedules and routines (the "lived" curriculum).

Conventional curriculum practices largely ignore the questions of "whose values" should be propagated in the schools, and because they are almost never questioned, the existing power relationships in the larger society into which schools fit are reinforced and extended by such practices. Figure 2.3 is illustrative of this point.

C. Developing Curriculum Is a Political Activity and Not a Metaphysical Exercise

Knowledge is rarely neutral. The selection of knowledge to include in a school curriculum is fundamentally a political act of deciding who benefits from selecting what in the school's curriculum and who is excluded or diminished simultaneously. The curriculum in schools is a form of cultural capital, which is a form of aesthetic dispositions (taste, dress, manner of speaking, manners,

Figure 2.3   Selecting Curriculum Content

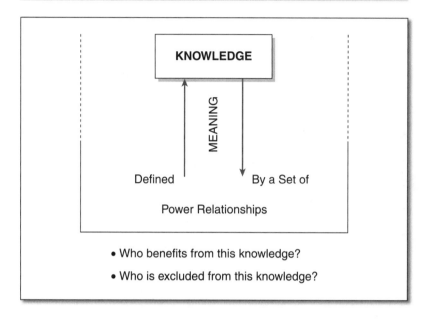

- Who benefits from this knowledge?
- Who is excluded from this knowledge?

what is worth knowing, etc.), which are often taken to be some "available to all on a equal basis and thus not recognized as the result of a specific process of cultural transmission and training that is in fact not available to all" (Johnson, 1993, p. 24).

A more accurate view of what is really going on in developing a curriculum is shown in Figure 2.4. Curriculum construction goes on in schools within the unspoken and dominant educational ideology: the dominant political ideology that serves as "hidden" screens for the actual process of writing the acceptable work plans in schools. Rarely are these screens made overt or completely understandable. For example, Shor (1986, pp. 104–194) avers that the national call for "excellence" and "high tech" are simply camouflaged strategies to maintain the existing political authority structure and inequality in the larger society. The Obama administration's "race to the top" can be similarly viewed because it assumes that everyone has equal access to the forms of cultural and social capital so such a "race" is "fair." Bernstein (1996) summarizes it this way, "There is likely to be an unequal distribution of images, knowledges, possibilities, and resources that will affect the rights of participation, inclusion, and individual enhancement of groups of students. It is highly likely that

Figure 2.4   Selecting Curriculum Content: The More Accurate View

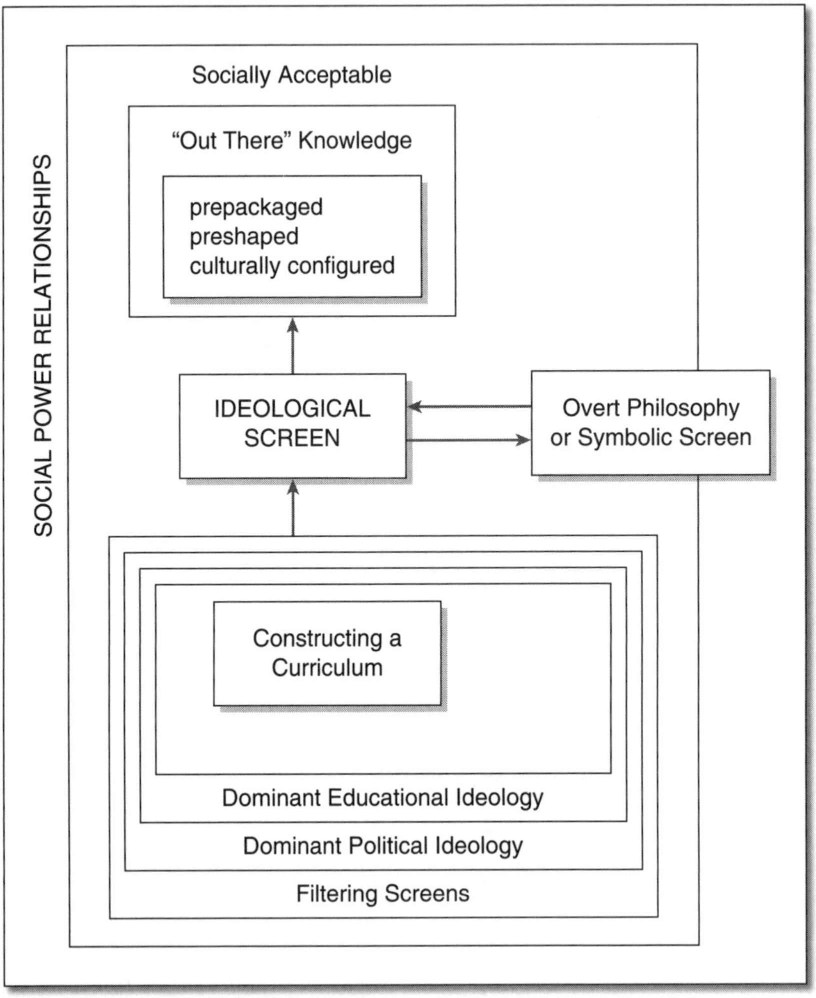

the students who do not receive these rights in the school come from social groups who do not receive these rights in society" (p. 8).

The "we believe" statements commonly "guiding" curriculum construction in most school districts are nothing more than *ideological political screens* to ensure that whatever is finally "developed" conforms to the ideology. After this, knowledge or content (the so-called facts) is selected to match this screen.

Because this is never a truly open-ended process, the knowledge "selected" really has been preselected, preshaped, to fit whatever the dominant cultural configuration happens to be at the time. When the process is passed off as "engineering" or "scientific," its real biases are submerged in a fake kind of "objective neutrality" that belies its essential subjectivity.

School curricula are almost never written from a philosophical base in day-to-day operations of local educational systems. At the state and national levels, in terms of problems in education, philosophy is rarely, if ever, applied. The reason is that true philosophy is highly abstract and quite generalized beyond a day-to-day arena of decision making or even a year-to-year one. Ideologies, on the other hand, as O'Neill has indicated (1981, p. 19) are much more specific and actually may direct social and political actions.

Because curriculum construction is aimed at directing educationally induced social and political actions, the outcomes are more accurately the product of an ideology as opposed to a philosophy. In addition, philosophies are much more apt to be concerned with processes and procedures as "protocols of inquiry" rather than a doctrine of belief. The "we believe's" of curriculum development are in fact statements of ideologies as opposed to philosophies.

2.2 Using a Needs Assessment to Develop a Curricular Framework

Curriculum development starts with a needs assessment, which is not a survey of faculty or parents about what they "need" in the schools. That kind of survey is merely a "perceptual inventory" of how people "feel" or "see" various programs and priorities that may or may not exist in the schools.

A needs assessment is a "gap analysis" of the *existing level of pupil performance* compared with *the desired level of pupil performance* (Kaufman & Herman, 1991, p. 140). To determine a need, the school administrator must have two indices present. The first is some tangible and measurable statement of outcomes that is valid and reliable. The second is a set of measurement instruments by which to assess the existing level of pupil performance compared with the desired levels. In neither case is a curriculum required because valid and reliable indicators or objectives are part of but not a whole curriculum, and a set of measurement tools may be part of but not a whole curriculum.

Obtaining a set of valid and reliable outcomes by which a needs assessment is performed is the first task of the educator in constructing curriculum.

A. Creating Valid and Reliable Educational Outcome Indicators

Generating a comprehensive list of valid and reliable outcome indicators is the first task in performing a needs assessment. Outcome indicators are discrete learner performance statements that are "macro" level in scope; that is, they represent the more or less final point of where learners should be or what they should know, feel, or do when the responsibilities of the school system are officially over. That means the outcome indicators are for 12th grade plus in K–12 school systems. One way to think about it is that, when a student steps forward to receive his or her high school diploma, what are the minimally essential skills, knowledge, and attitudes that he or she should possess?

One example might be this one, "At the conclusion of the 12th grade, the student will be able to read the editorial page of *The New York Times* with 100% accuracy and be able to point out instances of arguments not based on logic or fact."

This statement is very different than one that simply asserts, "At the end of the 12th grade, students will be able to think critically." This type of outcome statement is too global to be of very much use in performing a needs assessment because that process will require the selection of measurement tools to assess whether or not students can or do perform at the level required or implied in an outcome statement. If statements are as vague as the latter one, it is very hard to select an appropriate measurement tool or procedure. In such cases, the selection of the tool then really functions to define what was meant in the construction of the indicator. In this instance, the test or measurement tool becomes the indicator instead of independently measuring its attainment. For this not to happen, outcome indicators must be as specific as test content, or the test content becomes the substitute for the curriculum content and redefines the true meaning of the indicator itself.

It also ought to be clear that the selection of any set of indicators includes implicit and explicit values about culture. An indication of using the *New York Times* over say, *The Daily Racing Form* is loaded with values and is an expression of cultural capital (see Bourdieu, 1984).

B. The Curriculum Outcome Indicator Validation Matrix

The potential list of outcome indicators is nearly infinite, especially when one considers the limited amount of pupil time available for schooling, which is between 14,000 and 15,000 hours, K–12. The rate of knowledge known to human kind is doubling every two to five years, which increases the pressures on selecting indicators and subsequent content that are indeed "most valuable."

One method to select the most appropriate curriculum outcome indicators is to construct a curriculum outcome validation matrix. The matrix is shown in Table 2.1.

The matrix is simply a listing of groups or persons considered to be critical in determining agreement with any proposed set of outcome indicators. There can be as many as required or desired.

Table 2.1   A Sample Curriculum Content Validation Matrix

Proposed Content to Be Included in the Curriculum	State Law	National Task Force	State Test	Local Policy	Local Teacher Poll	Textboo	Futurists
Content (however defined)	Reference all applicable provisions of existing state law to the proposed content in this column.	Refer specifically to task force reports in content areas such as the NCTM, AAAS, NCTE, and the like.	Perform an initial review of the alignment of the content of the state test(s) and the proposed content for your curriculum.	Refer to relevant local policy requirements or adopted outcome goals.	This column can refer to priorities of teachers regarding possible content inclusion.	Reference existing and proposed textbook content to proposed content in this column.	Use selected futurists to establish trends that your graduates will face
Processes							
Skills							
Attitudes							
Concepts							
Other							

The listing under the "proposed content" column can be in any form desired so long as it is specific enough to relate to the references and the tests that will be used to assess them. The outcome indicators can be in the form of content to be learned or processes, skills, attitudes, or concepts to be acquired.

In this context, *validation* means simply the attainment of consensus of the referent groups or persons used in the matrix. School officials will have to set the level of consensus; that is, how many "yes" or "matches" actually constitute consensus and whether all groups or persons are counted with the same weight.

The most common referents used in curriculum validation are state law and regulations, state tests, local board policies or requirements, textbook references, national curricular task forces, recommendations from national educational curriculum organizations (such as the National Council of Teachers of Mathematics or the National Council of Teachers of English), local teachers, and futurists.

Futurists are an important source to validate proposed curriculum outcome indicators if educators argue that the curriculum will prepare students to function in a world that as yet does not exist. Such futurists identify key trends that will have an impact on the lives of the students in their times.

For example, if this new century is the "Asian Century" as so many have predicted with the locus of the world's development shifting to the Pacific Rim, what should school curricula include to prepare students to work and live successfully in this world? (See Cetron & Gayle, 1991, pp. 93–128.) Already the three biggest banks in the world are located in China and over 7,000 Chinese companies are functioning or investing all over the globe. In fact, even with the world's economic downturn, China will account for "as much as 60% of global growth" (Medeiros, 2009, p. 254). Among the other fastest growing world economies is Vietnam (Walder, 2009). And while North Korea is on economic life support, militarily it remains bellicose, bent on developing nuclear weapons and test firing a long-range missile into the sea shortly after President Obama had begun his term of office (Cumings, 2009).

Despite such economic and military "facts," the answer is not simple because it is influenced by one's "ideology." If the curriculum developer is a political conservative, he or she may simply say, "Educate a student in the basic liberal arts and he or she will know how to confront any situation." If a curriculum developer is more liberal, he or she may say, "Asian culture and the Chinese language should replace the heavy emphasis on the European culture and Latin."

Actually, the curriculum matrix proposes an eclectic response in which all of the opinions are factored into making this determination.

It should be noted, however, that almost all available sources are politically and educationally conservative in outlook. Citizen polls, state legislatures, national task forces, and tests as well as boards of education will reflect a dominant emphasis on the status quo or the past because that is the frame of reference of most of the respondents in the matrix. Emerging social needs usually run far ahead of the perception of those working in schools, which helps explain why much of the curriculum is outdated. A standing joke in social studies is that it is nearly always "one war behind."

Once the validation matrix is constructed and the groups and persons are invited to indicate their agreement or disagreement, then the results are tabulated. Each person or group is allowed one vote (a "yes" or a "no" vote). The level of agreement may be set at 90%, in which case a level of consensus that is lower than that would not be considered for inclusion into a school or school district's list of outcome indicators. Respondents may "rank" the potential outcome indicators on several scales connoting importance. In this case, numerical averages are computed to show high and low ones as an index of perceived group and overall importance.

It should be noted that the development of these general district indicators is not located within any particular curriculum content area; that is, they do not represent a discipline so that the indicators are "out of discipline." Curriculum content areas (math, science, language arts, and so on) are simply convenient grouping points or "organizing centers" for curriculum content considered similar or comparable.

If one only develops outcome indicators in math, for example, the inclusion of "math" is a foregone conclusion in the subsequent development of curriculum. This option also forecloses locating an outcome indicator in some other area of the curriculum that may be more appropriate.

For example, "balancing a checkbook" could be ranked as an outcome indicator in math. Or it could be an indicator in home economics or even social studies. Once it is ranked as a "math" outcome indicator, however, the option for locating it elsewhere may be foreclosed.

For curriculum developers to have maximum latitude to locate outcome indicators in the most appropriate content area, outcome indicators should be listed initially without regard to the curriculum discipline in which they traditionally may be found.

C. Selecting the Measurement
Tools to Determine Pupil Performance

Remembering that a needs assessment is a gap analysis between the desired level of pupil performance and the actual level of performance, pupil attainment must now be assessed in relationship to the outcome indicators.

What this means is that a test or tests must be selected that really match the outcome indicators so that a score derived from the test is considered an appropriate measure of the actual level of pupil learning on a specific outcome indicator.

Tests, therefore, have to be aligned with the outcome indicators. A combination of tests and other types of assessments can be used as well as homegrown tests to determine how well pupils have learned that which is required for them to do well on the outcome indicators.

In some cases, the outcome indicators will have to be broken down into smaller pieces and tested at grade levels earlier than the 12th grade. The process of defining the outcome indicators into smaller components is largely one of logical extrapolation in which the requisite subskills and knowledge are delineated (see Glatthorn, 1987, pp. 143–159).

Test reliability is generally known for commercially prepared batteries and to some extent for statewide instruments. For locally developed criterion-referenced tests or teacher-made tests, reliability will have to be established. Although there are several forms of determining test reliability, the Kuder-Richardson test item approach is a standard procedure often used for this purpose (see Payne, 1968, pp. 129–140). Computer programs for using the KR-20 are available for purchase and use in school systems.

Once the tests and other assessments have been given to the students and the scores compiled, then the actual needs assessment process can begin. The needs assessment is simply a list of gaps or discrepancies between desired and actual levels of pupil performance in a school or a school district.

Gaps or "needs" are usually listed by size and by indicator priority. For example, suppose 29% of the students could not read and interpret that editorial in *The New York Times*. That gap may not be as important as noting that 42% of the graduating seniors could not recognize the opening strains of Beethoven's "Fifth Symphony." Although the music "need" is larger, it may not have the same importance as the one in reading and interpretation of expository prose.

2.3 CONSTRUCTING CURRICULUM WITH GAP DATA

The gap or "need" data can be used to construct or adapt a curriculum. Remembering that a curriculum is a type of work plan, the discrepancy data can be attached to places in the existing curriculum or textbook series where skills, knowledge, and attitudes are supposed to be taught. This act simply reconnects the needs assessment data back to the work plan in whatever form it exists. As the curriculum constructors examine the reconnection, they should be searching to see whether the learning discrepancies are the result of inadequacies in the work plan.

For example, suppose that, in trying to improve the number of students who can read *The New York Times* properly, the curriculum developers discover that the curriculum has very few examples like the one outcome indicator on which they are being tested. By moving to expand this area in the curriculum, they ensure that many more students may pass that item on subsequent tests. The alteration of the work plan is part of curriculum development.

In case there is no work plan of any kind, a curriculum is constructed by arraying the outcome indicators and their requisite subskills into the logical descending order to be taught. In this way, needs assessment data that are largely descriptive become a prescription. If such subskills and knowledge are to be taught repetitively in greater sophistication with subsequent grades, a spiral curriculum is the result. Repetition in teaching is not only a function of ensuring mastery (a delivery concern) but of building into the curriculum the necessary reinforcement (a curriculum design problem; see Gagne & Briggs, 1979).

Figure 2.5 shows the progression of curriculum development generally followed in many school systems. Beginning with the construction of an ideology and the derivation of outcome indicators and subsequent tests, gaps become the basis of the construction of curriculum (the needs assessment). In turn, revealed gaps are located in curricular subjects and then in courses of study. From these, smaller divisions of curriculum called "units" are created.

Figure 2.5   Traditional Curriculum Development Sequence

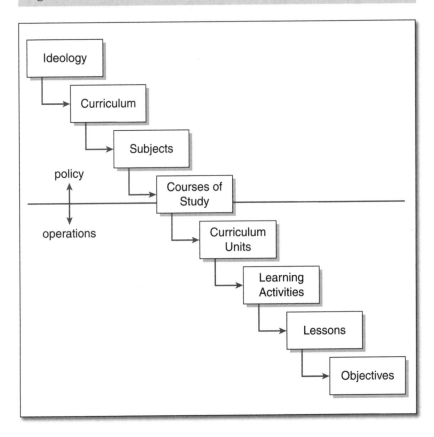

Within units, learning activities, objectives, and lesson plans carry the development of a detailed work plan to the classroom teacher to deliver (see McNeil, 1977, pp. 93–103).

2.4 CONSTRUCTING "USER FRIENDLY" CURRICULUM WORK PLANS

The legends about curriculum guides being "Manhattan telephone books," gathering dust in classroom corners and closets, are legion in the teaching profession. A veteran principal once commented to me, "I've been in this school district for 40 years, and in all that time, nobody ever stole a curriculum guide!" This anecdote epitomizes the lack of true utility such work plans often have for classroom teachers. Many are ponderous and of dubious validity. Often, they are not much more than "cut-and-paste" old textbooks that were glued together to satisfy the requirements for a little curriculum work for a couple of weeks of afternoon summer speculation. Why school districts continue to pay scarce taxpayer dollars for the construction of materials that are of marginal worth to the improvement of pupil learning remains one of the enduring mysteries of education. Perhaps they don't know any better. In other places, curriculum consists of scattered work documents such as state department frameworks, locally produced pacing guides, or standard courses of study and/or commercially prepared worksheets.

To improve the quality of curricular work plans, we must examine some of the regnant myths about them.

A. Myth 1: "Bubble-Up" Curriculum Approaches Are Best to Ensure Teacher Loyalty

One of the great fallacies that permeates the curriculum field is the notion about the requirement for teachers to develop their own curriculum or work plans. The rationale goes that, if they don't actually write it, they don't or won't "own it," and if they don't "own it," it will all come to naught (see Taba, 1962, p. 469).

This myth ignores the fact that most teachers are far more loyal to their textbooks than to curriculum guides, even when they wrote the guides. Teacher loyalty is given to those materials that *really work with children*. The matter of who wrote them is quite secondary. The bulk of materials used by most teachers is material they did not write themselves. It is, however, quite true that while teachers may not have written their work plans, they have considerable leeway in selecting those they feel are effective with their children. That is an important point. Ownership means making a personal decision about "what works" and having the professional power to keep using those things that work and to expand them.

B. Myth 2: The State Is Always Right in the Selection of Curriculum Content and the Role of the Teacher Is to be Compliant in Accepting It

Much of the curriculum literature is filled with pictures of teachers pondering the future of the world, working to develop curriculum that helps children move into the future. The fact is that teachers work under an enormous set of constraints in developing curriculum.

The intrusion of state law and new requirements most often in the form of mandates for subject matter or sequencing; state testing programs that are politically motivated and administered to reveal "deficit schools or school systems," of which, by definition, nearly 50% are conceded to be at the outset by the logic of the statistical machinery employed and textbook adoptions that also standardize the curriculum—all must somehow be taken into account.

To develop a curriculum that ignores these powerful forces would be to create an irrelevant document few actually reference. So teachers cannot act in isolation in developing curriculum. They must acknowledge the power and influence other groups in U.S. society possess in setting the context in which curriculum development is undertaken. The authorization of teachers to write curriculum always occurs within a specified legal-social-political context in which schools must function.

Yet this fact cannot ignore the delicate balance that exists in this special organizational space where teachers work. We not only expect teachers to be dutiful agents of an approved curriculum, but we also expect them to be aware of the necessity of their continuing professional judgments and of their social consciousness and aware-ness of how their work fits in to the larger social mores and values of the society schools support and reproduce. It is the social repro-duction of the larger society where conflict and tension most often arise as it pertains to schools and the curriculum in them.

If there are injustices in the larger society and our own history provides ample evidence of their existence overt the life of the nation, what role do the schools have in challenging and changing them? When slavery was legal, did school teachers challenge its existence in the conduct of their duties? When women were denied the right to vote, did school curricula contain challenges to the assumptions of female inferiority? When schools were segregated, did not that mere fact of that segregation reinforce second class cit-izenship for African Americans? How many schools took indepen-dent steps to integrate themselves?

Our social history provides ample evidence that teachers, adminis-trators, and school curricula buttress the existing social class structure of privilege and power along whatever lines exist at the time. In retro-spect, to take steps to make schools more efficient in the perpetuation of these now discredited social beliefs and practices appears absurd, and yet we continue to largely follow contemporary social practices that may ultimately contain similar injustices with improved assessment and alignment, *unless we position them within the larger context of school and society.* When Ida Wells Barnett (1862–1931), a public school teacher in Memphis, Tennessee, wrote articles in the local paper about the inadequacies of schools for black children, she lost her job to continue teaching in the Memphis schools. Today, there would be few who would not support Barnett and her outrage, but there were none in her own time, and justice went begging in Memphis. We will speak more on this topic in Chapter 4.

C. Myth 3: Curriculum Should Be Developed Independently of Textbooks and Tests

Traditionally, curriculum has been viewed as a separate kind of effort to produce a uniquely local work plan. The rationale is that localized curriculum should not be influenced by textbooks or tests. The notion is that curriculum should *lead* and *not follow.*

What is often forgotten in this approach is that, if a school or school district releases many different kinds of work plans to teachers, the designers have some obligation to determine which is the best and the intercorrelation between them. This should be a primary objective in the creation of work plans because teachers have the option of choosing which one to use in most cases.

On the other hand, once curriculum is seen as one of a number of different types of work plans that may exist in a school, then its relationships to the other work plans that may exist becomes an important consideration. The so-called primacy of localized curriculum usually only exists in the head of the superintendent or chief curriculum officer. Such primacy is often nonexistent out in the schools as textbooks continue to dominate classroom teaching as the major work plan (see Apple, 1986).

The other "myth" is that those who construct the curriculum should maintain a "blind eye" to what is tested. This posture prevents those constructing the work plan from understanding how and what will be measured. It would be similar to determining to build some kind of product and not having any idea of how the quality of the item would be assessed for fear that somehow the assessment process itself would somehow be damaged.

If the assessment is indeed measuring the desired work to be done, then the assessment criteria should be the same as for the item itself. The only way assessment data are useful to improve the actual work going on is through ensuring that the work being assessed is the work desired to be accomplished. These issues will be discussed in greater detail in Chapter 3 on alignment.

D. Myth 4: Pacing Guides and State Guidelines Replace the Need for Local Curricula

Because the capacity of local school systems is very limited due to personnel shortages to actually write good local curricula, especially in small districts, the administration determines that they will use the state guidelines or framework and simply develop *pacing guides* to ensure that everything that gets taught is within those official documents. The danger here is that *pacing guides* may standardize the one thing that should remain nonstandardized in high-stakes testing scenarios, that is, the necessary variation within classrooms required for teachers to truly differentiate instruction. The second problem is that even if a *pacing guide* is constructed with high global alignment to a state framework, rarely are such state documents sufficiently specific to really account for possible ranges of variance due to content ambiguity. About the best that can be said for *pacing guides* is that they create the means to check to determine if the recommended state curriculum can actually be taught in the time available and before the actual test is administered. They thus offer some assurance at a very simplistic level of a form of crude alignment. However, this modest advantage can more than be offset by the instructional rigidity it may impose on school classrooms making it difficult for teachers to adjust curriculum content to actual learning pace and discouraging teachers from differentiating instruction in the name of adhering to arbitrarily imposed lesson times. The bottom line is there is no substitute for a good, specific, valid, aligned, local curriculum.

2.5 Moving From Curriculum Content to Work Tasks

After curriculum validation occurs, the next task is to transpose the most highly ranked content into a form that makes it easily translated into the classroom. This means that content must be stated in the form of work tasks for the teacher. A good way of thinking about this problem is to pose these questions:

- The teacher is to do what?
- Under what conditions?
- With what tools or materials?
- To attain what results?

Typically, many curriculum guides begin by stating the work tasks for the teacher as a "behavioral" objective (see Mager, 1962). This is a mistake. First, behavioral objectives are not statements of teacher work tasks, they are statements of *work measurement* (English, 1987, p. 193). Behavioral objectives indicate what students are to do, not what teachers should be teaching. If behavioral objectives are going to be used in a curriculum guide, they should be used in a section pertaining to evaluation (Armstrong, Cornell, Kraner, & Roberson, 1970).

The way to state teacher tasks is to focus on actions that the teacher should be taking with the specified content. See the following example:

During a discussion of famous American women who were minorities, introduce the case of Lucy Gonzales Parsons, one of the first Chicanas to make a significant contribution to the American labor movement. Present the status of American labor in the late nineteenth century that led to the Haymarket Massacre. Show the students how Lucy Gonzales Parsons' work led to the establishment of the eight-hour day. (Mirande & Enriquez, 1979, p. 88)

Another way to state the work of the teacher would be the following: "Present the life of Lucy Gonzales Parsons as an exemplar of early American feminism among minorities. Have the students perform library research on her life and develop several vignettes for a small playlet for performance for the class."

Exactly how much detail should be present in a curriculum guide regarding teacher work tasks *depends* upon (a) the sophistication and knowledge of the staff, (b) the type of content that has been selected, (c) the extent of dependence of the staff upon access to critical facilities (labs, libraries, computers, and so on), (d) the presence and availability of appropriate materials such as textbooks and other supplementary materials, (e) the expectations of achievement as embodied in local, state, or national tests and exams, and (f) the range and diversity of the pupil population and any special requirements they may possess to engage in successful learning.

In one scenario, let us suppose that "School District A" is a rapidly growing but older school system near an inner city in the southwest. There has been high teacher turnover and a large percentage of the faculty is composed of newcomers to teaching. They meet students who are coming from poor neighborhoods with all the attendant problems associated with poverty. Although some of the school buildings are modem, they are not stocked well with books and supplementary materials. The state has recently initiated a testing program in which large numbers of students have performed poorly. If the poor pupil performance continues, the district faces possible sanctions.

The curriculum guide developed for School District A will contain much more explicit information for young, inexperienced faculty than if the faculty were seasoned and successful veterans. The guides will contain many more references that entail methodological work tasks (how to present something) than not. Connections from the content to the students will reference ways teachers can create materials not available to them because of the lack of adequate supplementary materials. And the presence of the state-imposed and mandatory testing program means that critical *alignment* information should be included in the guides to ensure maximum pupil performance. Guides should be rich with alignment data regarding examples of how students will be assessed and also show sample question formats. Recommended time ranges should be present to help an inexperienced faculty focus on the highest priorities with the students.

Now take "School District B." This is a wealthy suburban school system with experienced teachers who are quite stable. Likewise, the student population is very stable and well off. Scores on state tests are high and responsive to state criteria. The curriculum guide for School District B is likely to be leaner, smaller, and cryptic. It might even be in the form of a one-page checklist reminder format.

Functional work plans fit the situation. They enable the faculty to quickly focus on the essentials, make the necessary connections, relate essential learning to the school environment, and maximize pupil success, however locally defined.

2.6 CONSTRUCTING "USER FRIENDLY" CURRICULUM GUIDES

"User friendly" curriculum guides emphasize the development of well-organized, easy to read, unambiguous textual language that is contextually relevant to real classrooms and real procedures. "Pie-in-the-sky" platitudes, elaborate philosophies, academic rhetoric or research mumbo jumbo, long lists of excessively technical performance objectives, numerous footnotes and quotations, and the like should be eliminated from functional work plans as they assume the form of a curriculum guide.

Textbook companies spend millions trying to perfect the process of translation from the book to the classroom. As a reminder, pick out a textbook that teachers in your building enjoy using and examine the *Teacher's Guide.* The probability is quite good that what you will see are "simple and lean" "user friendly" directions and examples that make it easy to move from a desired state to one present in a classroom. Modern textbooks might be vapid on content (a charge frequently heard), but they are far superior to any yet produced as examples of effective work plans that actually can *be taught as written.*

Functional curriculum guides take into account the work situation, the nature of the teachers and students, relevant expectations as embodied in law, and evaluation procedures (tests). They enable teachers to tie together the important elements of being "in control" of the classrooms in which they work.

"User friendly" curriculum guides are *stand-alone* documents; that is, they require no other document to understand, interpret, or refer to in order to "tighten" the curriculum (written, taught, and tested) if desired. "User friendly" curriculum guides are well indexed; cross referencing by topic and problem is easy. It is possible for a veteran teacher to "get into" and "get out of" a guide quickly and easily without having to read the whole thing.

"User friendly" curriculum guides are small. They fit into purses and pockets easily. They do not resemble huge, three-ring binders that discourage teachers from using them.

2.7 ESSENTIAL ELEMENTS IN CURRICULUM GUIDES

It is quite conceivable in some situations that all a curriculum guide might contain would be a listing of the required content to be taught (in whatever form the "content" assumes). That would be all that would be required in some circumstances where pupil performance was deemed to be adequate and no "tightening" was necessary.

What, however, can a district and its staff do if this is not the case? Suppose that a school district's test scores or other measures of academic learning are not deemed to be adequate. What can be done? If the district only has a checklist type of curriculum guide, the data base will not be adequate to improve pupil performance.

In this case, the district will have to reconstruct its work plans to enable it to more fully concentrate its resources to improve pupil performance. The purpose of a functional curriculum guide is to *focus* and *connect* the work of teachers.

Tests, no matter what kind and no matter where administered, *assume* some kind of common experience to be possible in some sort of sequence, or else a comparison of one score with another would be impossible—lest scores assume the presence of a continuous variable (see Allen & Yen, 1979, p. 20). Commonality is a necessary assumption that must be present to connote meaning in any score compared with another. If every test score were totally idiosyncratic (i.e., one time only and absolutely unique), it would be ludicrous to make judgments on the basis of comparisons. Tests will always be an important variable in constructing curriculum, whether they come *after* or *before* curriculum. (These options will be pursued in greater detail in Chapter 3.)

The curriculum-test connection should be represented in a curriculum guide so that the classroom teacher knows what will be tested, when, and with what instruments. This connection can be as simple as that shown in Table 2.2, where "0" means a match with the tests, and "X" connotes a match with the curriculum and the test (this would be content alignment only).

A standardized norm-referenced test presents scores on the basis of how well a student performed compared with all of the other students who took a test. A criterion-referenced test reports a score on how many student answers were correct or incorrect. A common kind of criterion-referenced test many adults have taken and passed is the state driver's test.

Table 2.2   Representing the Curriculum–Test Connection in
Curriculum Guides

Curriculum Objective	Scope of Test Used		
	NRT	STATE CAP	DISTRICT CRT
1. Ability to infer the author's purpose, point of view, in a literary work	O	O	X
2. Ability to distinguish facts from normative statements	O	X	X
3. Can recognize cause-effect relationships	X	X	X
4. Can predict trends from given data	X	O	O
5. Can identify value judgments in various texts	O	O	X
6. Knowledge of early civilizations	X	X	O
7. Understands at least two nonmajority cultures in the United States	O	X	O
8. Ability to relate a story in personal terms	O	O	O
9. Can pick out logical fallacies in arguments	O	O	X
10. Can indicate from a TV advertisement various forms of propaganda in use	O	O	X
Totals	3	4	6

NOTE: NRT = the norm-referenced test used in the school system. STATE CAP = the state achievement test. DISTRICT CRT = the school system's criterion-referenced test.

From this sample of the 10 curricular objectives, the district's own criterion-referenced test would have the highest content alignment, followed by the state achievement test and the norm-referenced test. Teachers should know which tests will assess what curricular objectives *and the format that will be used to assess them* (context alignment). A detailed discussion regarding test ethics will be pursued in the next chapter.

The curriculum guide should indicate what should be taught (and also what will or should be learned), how what is to be taught or learned will be assessed—and by which instrument and when—and curricular objectives should be keyed to the textbooks teachers may use to implement the designated curricular objectives (by page number).

The keying of the textbook and the curriculum in this fashion means that as teachers are following the curriculum, they will be *moving around* the textbook and not teaching merely Chapter 1, 2, 3, and 4 in that order. For curricula to dominate and lead textbooks, the essential data teachers require should be present in the most easily translatable form possible. Unless the textbook pages are present, most teachers will not take the time to look them up, finally putting the guide aside and following the sequence of the test instead of the sequence of the curriculum.

Many school systems are also placing videocassettes, audiocassettes, films, filmstrips, and other aides by topic in curriculum guides next to curricular objectives. In this way, teachers know very quickly not only where various curricular objectives can be located in all of the textbooks but also what other resources contain the curricular objectives that must be taught and learned.

Finally, there must be some sort of time designation within the curriculum guide as to how much stress (in some convenient unit of time) is required to teach the designated objectives (or topics, subjects, themes, facts, processes, or the like).

The time designation is a prickly issue with teacher committees. Teachers often are reluctant to designate any time at all for fear it will be turned around and employed as an evaluative tool against them. For example, if they indicate that two periods should be spent on "applying context clues to determine meaning" in literature, experience will indicate that some students will take less than two periods and many may take considerably more. What then is the value of the designation if not to evaluate teacher efficiency?

The value of the time designation is considerably enhanced if the time is represented as ranges of time instead of *fixed units*. When provided with *ranges of time* based on pupil learning, teachers can receive some idea of the overall emphasis to be obtained and gain some idea as to how long it should take them to teach a concept, process, skill, fact, or the like.

Work plans without time specifications are nearly useless in eliminating the near universal teacher complaint about home-grown curriculum guides: "There's too much to teach in too little time to teach it in." This is a rather simple time-work problem familiar to industrial engineers. What makes development of practical work plans very difficult in schools is that while *time is a constant,* the curriculum is considered *variable* (i.e., expansive and flexible).

U.S. curriculum practice has been replete with numerous "add-ons" throughout its history (Kliebard, 1985, pp. 31–44). The practice continues into modem times with calls for such things as "global education," "education about AIDS," "student wellness," and many more. Such "add-ons" are rarely calculated in terms of their impact on other things in the curriculum as the convenient assumption is made that *somehow everything will fit!* Asking classroom teachers whether or not that assumption is true often can be a rude awakening to central office curriculum supervisors.

As a kind of work plan, curriculum should "fit" the time available for teachers to teach it. One of the reasons for the pervasive cynicism among teachers as to the real worth of curriculum guides is that they are not a "help" but "more work"; that is, they make the teachers' jobs more difficult not easier. The attitude of cynicism is the result of decades of production of voluminous often vapid and tedious tomes that are not "user friendly" and do not assist teachers in setting priorities within the actual time constraints of the day.

Most often, curriculum guides assume there is more time to teach than is actually present because they do not account for the numerous and unplanned interruptions teachers face—the necessity to collect and distribute things to children from lunch tickets to advertisements from booster groups, to take roll, and a host of other noninstructional chores that consume time allotted to teaching the content contained in the official curriculum guides of the district or school. Much of classroom teacher time is devoted to mechanical tasks imposed by the system that bear little relation to improving classroom instruction.

Too often, curriculum guides assume teachers possess a form of control that simply does not exist. For example, the impact of "pull-outs" at the elementary level severely hampers the capability of teaching the required curriculum with some of the students absent.

2.8 SETTING CONTENT PRIORITIES AND EXPRESSING TIME VALUES

Establishing time values within a curriculum and resolving the matter of how to get everything in that is deemed to be of "high" value requires the setting of priorities. Priorities can be established *before* a curriculum is written in the form of an ideology, or they can be developed *after* curriculum is written. There are strengths and weaknesses in either approach.

Setting the curriculum to a stated ideology ensures that the curriculum "fits" the ideology. Because much of what constitutes an ideology is "hidden" or implicit, the *before* model may be naive. It allows those hidden values and assumptions to remain unexpressed but dominant in the process. For example, to indicate that all children will pass a math test for demonstrated proficiency at a given level means that the statement accepts the content of the math test as appropriate, the values expressed in the content of the math questions as legitimate, and the role of the school in "teaching" that curriculum as viable. These are passed on without question in drafting a curriculum to meet this statement or standard.

All of these assumptions remain hidden or largely unexamined because they are accepted without question. In "front-end" curriculum work—the traditional approach in which philosophy-ideology is written first as a kind of preamble—the major weakness is that it reinforces the status quo because it fails to examine it at all. And the process tends to select means (curriculum) to match unexamined ends (assumed content and its values).

If the ideology or philosophy is written after the development of curriculum outcomes or indicators, then the creation or development of it can be deeply probed to reveal what the "real" values may be compared with the desired outcomes. This makes the development of the so-called rationale for curriculum much more public.

For example, after writing a curriculum indicator as "the desire to obtain a given score on a state math test," the question can be asked, "What are we really saying or meaning when this test and its content *become* our curriculum?" What are the implicit values and assumptions that *lie behind* this process? What is included on the test? What has been excluded from the test?

The approach of identifying the ideology *after* the curriculum outcomes are developed can be a useful but still flawed approach for setting priorities and the content of the curriculum. The flaw is that without thinking about the values and assumptions *before writing* the curriculum, the indicators or outcome statements developed will contain value judgments that become self-reinforcing if an ideology is written that "reflects" the hidden biases of the outcome indicators.

Whatever values are contained in the outcome indicators, in turn, become the umbrella ideology. The question could be asked, "Where in this cycle are the excluded values and assumptions not part of the indicators considered?" If probing questions are not asked at all, it matters little whether the development of the real ideology happens first before curriculum is written or in the middle after indicators are developed.

Curriculum is always a means to somebody's end. The end is the state's, the school system's, the teacher's, or the board's. Somebody has a vested interest in whatever outcomes or content are designated. This means that behind every curriculum is a set of power relationships that are reinforced or not reinforced by any given curriculum.

From this perspective, no selection of curriculum content ever can be considered a politically neutral act. The selection of curriculum content is always a political process because it involves the designation of a body of knowledge that reinforces the existing or changing set of power relationships in the school or the larger society (see Bourdieu & Passeron, 2000; Schubert, 1986, pp. 140–160).

Various constituencies have a vested interest in the maintenance of any given set of power relationships. Those in power are loath to relinquish it or to countenance any activity or process that would seriously disturb or diminish it.

Asking questions, for example, about which groups or people have the most to gain or lose in society with the maintenance or change in any given curriculum means that one is probing for the linkages between the perpetuation of some knowledge at the expense of other types of knowledge. It is also illustrative of how curriculum development is intimately a political activity interlinked with an educational one. Bourdieu (1984) talks about the interconnectedness between social capital, economic capital, and cultural capital as a sort of three-dimensional space which in varying degrees differentiate among the major classes for the conditions of existence (p. 114). The idea of narrowing something to be learned to one set of content represents an imposition, a "cultural arbitrary."

This is why such writings as Hirsch's (1988) *Cultural Literacy* are a hoax if passed off as a politically neutral (unbiased) activity. All knowledge benefits somebody and places someone else at a disadvantage. Bernstein (1996) talks about the school as a distributing place for images, a kind of ideology and asks the questions, "Who recognizes themselves as of value? What other images are excluded by the dominant image of value so that some students are unable to recognize themselves?" (p. 7) The procedure that follows is straight forward, but these questions need to be asked throughout the process, "Whose voice is heard? Who is speaking? Who is hailed by this voice? For whom is it familiar?" (Bernstein, 1996, p. 7).

To arrive at a system of priorities in selecting content, a simple sorting procedure can be used to eliminate much time-consuming discussion at the front end of curriculum development.

Teachers are asked, "What skills, knowledge, processes, attitudes, or [whatever content] should students possess after they leave Chemistry I, U.S. History, fifth-grade math, or home economics?" Each topic or outcome is placed on a 3×5 index card, with one topic per card. At this point, the topics do not have to be developed into so-called behavioral objectives.

After each teacher has completed a set of cards, a general meeting is held to sort them. The first teacher might lead off by saying, "A concept that is most important in history is the role of geography in shaping people's attitudes and culture." Suppose that of five teachers, all five agreed. All of the cards are grouped into one stack with a numerical value of five. The teacher continues with the others placing their cards in piles of fives, fours, threes, twos, and, if only one teacher has a concept, process, fact, or the like, then it is a singleton or one.

When the first teacher is out of cards, then the next teacher calls out his or her remaining cards, and they are sorted into fours, threes, twos, and singletons. This continues until all teachers are out of cards.

At this point, the piles (fives, fours, threes, twos, and ones) are simply typed up and returned to the faculty. Because it is the "fives" that all teachers have included, this represents the "consensus" curriculum. There should be a discussion, however, about what didn't make it to the list of "fives." Teachers may wish to argue for the inclusion or exclusion of topics or objectives about which they feel strongly. In this discussion, the real consensus is hammered out. Topics that finally are included on the "fives" are candidates for inclusion in the curriculum to be developed.

One early way to determine whether the "fives" fit the available time is to perform a rough time approximation check. The procedure works this way.

Potential curriculum topics are placed in priority order (again by consensus), from first to last. Then the teachers estimate the amount of time it would take to successfully teach their children so that 90% or more actually learned the topic, objective, process, or fact. The time estimates are cast as the *least amount of time* to the *most amount of time*. An example is shown in Table 2.3.

In this example, time is expressed in ranges instead of as fixed points. The ranges have been established by the faculty based on their experience in teaching the topics with the students in the school(s) in which they work. A range of 1.5 to 3.0 means that, based on the teachers' actual experience, they have been able to reach mastery for 90% of their students in between 1.5 to 3.0 instructional periods.

When the "least amount of time" column is summed, the total number of class periods should not exceed the total possible in a quarter, semester, or year (whatever the official length of time is for the class), or *there is too much curriculum for the real time available.*

The "least amount of time" column represents an *ideal,* that is, *when everything goes right!* Because this does not occur very often, the actual amount of time is going to be more than was estimated. The "most amount of time" column essentially should be seen in terms of Murphy's Law; that is, given the likelihood that

Table 2.3   Establishing Time Ranges for Topics in Instructional
Periods for Physical Geography

Potential Priority Topics	Shortest	Longest Time
1. Earth, sun, and moon	1.5	3.0
2. The plan of the Earth	1.0	3.0
3. World economy	3.0	7.0
4. The land	2.0	4.0
5. Gradation of running water	1.5	4.5
6. Economic relations of streams	1.0	5.5
7. Gradation by ice	3.5	4.5
8. Standing water	3.0	4.0
9. Gradation by ground water and wind	and so on	and so on
10. Soils		
11. The sea		
12. Coasts and ports		
13. The atmosphere		
14. Moisture in the air		
15. Climate		
16. Plant region		
17. Geography of animals		
18. The human species		
Totals		

everything could go wrong, it does! In these cases, the time
expressed will be more toward the maximum. But the designation
of the time ranges means that at least 90% of the students can (and
have) attained mastery in some time between these two numerical
expressions.

The purpose of establishing the time ranges is to force the curriculum developers to confront the actual time issue teachers really face when trying to implement a curriculum with real children. The figure takes into account learning pace and other physical conditions that may be present in the school units in which teachers actually work. The time ranges should not be used to evaluate teachers. That is one of the fears teachers have in placing any estimate of time in a curriculum work plan.

If the principal is going to come into a classroom and "dock" a teacher for taking more time than that expressed in the curriculum work plan, teachers rightly refuse to provide any estimate of the expected time it might take to effectively deliver any curriculum. Time ranges force curriculum developers to create work plans that can be taught in the real time and conditions confronting teachers in their classrooms and schools.

Time ranges force curriculum developers (who may be teachers) to develop work plans that are realistic. The practice of facing the time and content priority issue nearly always reduces the size of curriculum guides. It reduces the "wish list" curriculum to one that is "realistic" and most likely to become the taught curriculum.

2.9 A WORD ABOUT SEQUENCE AND STRESS

The reader can tell from the table on physical geography that the topics are listed in numerical order. This "order" constitutes the *sequence* established for teaching physical geography. The order established in most curriculum guides is largely arbitrary, that is, more a product of being "logical" as opposed to being inherently "psychological." Most curricular sequences have more to do with gauging what should be taught first for the desired outcomes to be reached that involve those things (or topics, content) to be used later or toward the end of teaching.

Tests also establish curricular sequence. Where tests are given, they establish points by which teachers and school systems work back to create a sequence of instruction that prepares students to take the test. A rationale for a test to be given usually involves the major decision-making points in the educational system and has little to do with learning theory or child development.

Curriculum sequence is most often the creature of some logical, developmental order created with an individual curriculum content area that makes sense to scholars and practitioners in that field. Few, if any, are theoretically *grounded* in proven psychology that can be translated to pedagogical principles. The state of the art in terms of learning is far from the precision required to enable that kind of translation.

Stress or emphasis in a curriculum pertains to the extent that the topic or content receives considered attention. It is assumed that more important topics receive more time within any curricular sequence than the less important ones. Time spent is an indication of importance as well as of complexity. It is possible that something may be maximally important but not very demanding to do. For example, learning to wear safety goggles in a shop class is vital but takes little time except for occasional reminders from the instructor to wear them.

Some things are presented again and again in a curriculum with increasing levels of complexity added. This is the concept of a *spiral* or expanding base within a curriculum. For example, primary students may learn the Pledge of Allegiance by rote. They are continually exposed to the ideas within the pledge so that at some point they come to understand the abstract idea contained in the phrase, "one nation indivisible," a concept few primary students grasp entirely until maturation and instruction come together to enable them to truly understand (see Hunkins, 1980, p. 234)

2.10 A Recommended Curriculum Guide Format

When constructing curricular work plans, "small is beautiful." In the past, educators have paid too little attention to simple things such as the ways curriculum could be presented to make it easy to reference, use, take home, and compare with lesson plans or state-produced testing materials.

The assumption in the past has been that the ubiquitous three-ring binder is the best way to package curriculum. That this may not be so may come as a surprise. Three-ring binders are often quite bulky and if they become too large, discourage teachers from taking them home to use in laying out units and lessons. The hidden message with three-ring binders is that the curriculum won't be around long enough to "bind" anyway, so don't spend too much time with it because it will be changed.

Too often, curriculum supervisors view the matter as perpetually engaging in curriculum development. Teachers, however, see it differently. Teachers are very "present oriented" as opposed to supervisors and principals who are "future oriented" (Wolcott, 1977). This fundamental difference between teachers and their supervisors is no more apparent than in the construction of curriculum guides. Teachers want something that is immediate, practical, applied, and "hands on." Curriculum guides too often are ethereal, vague, general-purpose outlines that defy practicality. One result is that, when alone behind their classroom walls, teachers junk the curriculum guide and reach for their textbooks.

A dog-eared curriculum guide ought to be enshrined as a paragon of virtue because it would mean that such documents were useful and referenced a lot. The idea is to make it easy to get curriculum guides out of bottom drawers, closets, and stacks of other papers by making them compact and accessible.

Curriculum guides ought to recognize that the teacher is the only person who can tie together the essential elements of internal system control or loosen as the situation requires, and the teacher usually does that task alone and without help. Few human organizations are so totally dependent upon a single person working in isolation from all others and without formal linkage to attain important work task flow connectivity and simultaneous flexibility.

A recommended curriculum guide format is shown in Table 2.4. It consists of a single sample page from a larger curricular document in any subject. It links the content to be taught to textbooks and other materials, contains important classroom cues (without getting into elaborate cookbook recipes), and links all of these facets to tests in use and sample test items to deal with all aspects of alignment. The time to be spent is stated in time ranges rather than as fixed points.

Curriculum guide formats can be horizontal or vertical, but they need to be concise, unambiguous, and lean. Constructing such documents is not a job most teachers have had much training with, and it is clearly beyond lesson plan development. These curriculum documents can be considered a kind of "meta lesson plan," a kind of grammar by which lesson plans can be constructed.

Table 2.4 A Sample Curriculum Guide Format That Maximizes Local Control of Textbooks and Tests

Content to Be Taught	Textbook(s): Reference by Page	Other Materials Referenced	Classroom Cues	Tests in Use	Sample Test Item(s)	Recommended Time Ranges
Content can be stated as topics, skills, processes, themes, facts, values, attitudes, and knowledge. It does not have to be stated in behavioral terms.	All textbooks that may be used should be listed and keyed by page to the first column. When teachers "follow" the guide, they should be moving around the textbooks rather than letting them "dictate" content and sequence.	All other extant supplementary materials should be keyed to Column 1, and their locations should be stated as follows: (s) = school based, and (crs) = central resource based.	Important cues by which the curriculum can be connected to classroom procedures or any special approach required to teach successfully should be indicated here.	This column should key each topic or objective to any text that will measure it. This is "content" alignment.	By showing actual text examples, "context" alignment information is provided. These data can also be connected to the "classroom cues" column.	Time ranges should be normed locally by experienced teachers and include the largest share of the population that is possible. Use periods or modules for secondary schools and minutes or hours for elementary schools.

NOTE: The size should be small and compact. Avoid making curriculum guides "cookbooks" of methods and recipes, which tends to greatly increase their size. Likewise, curriculum guides are not substitutes for the teacher's guide of a textbook series. Guides should tie together the written, taught, and tested curricula.

CHAPTER THREE

Aligning the Curriculum

*C*urriculum alignment refers to the "match" or overlap between the content, format, and level of cognition of the curriculum (or curriculum surrogate such as the textbook). The closer the fit or match is, the greater the potential for student improvement on the test. Another word for alignment is familiarity, which is why on nearly all assessments except diagnostic types practice leads to improvement because it enhances accuracy and speed of response

Figure 3.1 Curriculum Alignment: The Relationship Can Be Entered One of Two Ways

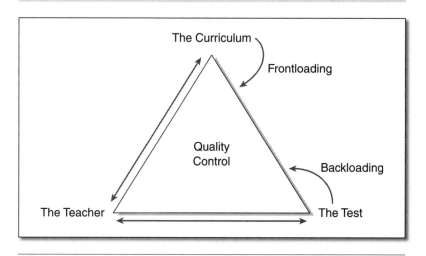

NOTE: Frontloading = establishing the "fit" by working form the curriculum to the test. Backloading = working from the test to the curriculum.

and reduces uncertainty or surprise on the part of the test-taker. It is why the alignment in classroom settings that are tested is sometimes referred to as "the doctrine of no surprises for children."

Curriculum alignment is therefore a process to improve the match between the formal instruction that occurs in the school and the classroom and that which any test will measure. Employing the model of curricular quality control of this book, Figure 3.1 shows two ways curriculum alignment can be established.

3.1 THE PROCESS OF ALIGNMENT BY FRONTLOADING

The first way curriculum alignment can be established is through a process called *frontloading*. This practice means that the educator writes his or her curriculum first and then searches for an appropriate test to measure or assess whether or not students have learned that which the curriculum includes. Frontloading is nearly universal in being preferred as a practice in schools because it establishes the primacy of the curriculum to which the test must follow and not lead. In this scenario, the test always follows the curriculum and does not "establish" it.

This is a sensitive issue with local educators, who often fear that teaching to or from the test raises the issue of who possesses the expertise to establish any curriculum as well as its propriety. The assumption is that local educators know best, though that is often not the case.

Local educators are also acutely sensitive to the fact that tests, particularly standardized tests, may represent an extremely narrow and rigid view of the actual goals and objectives of any local curriculum (see McNeil, 2000). Yeh (2001) has indicated that experts have criticized many state accountability tests that force teachers to "narrow the curriculum, focus on memorization, drills, and worksheets, and to reduce the already limited time available to focus on critical thinking skills" (p. 12). Teachers are extremely sensitive to this shortcoming of standardized tests, with a good many believing that such tests are inappropriate measures of the learning process (see Smith, 1991; Smith & Rottenberg, 1991).

A. Problems With Frontloading

Furthermore, locally developed tests are notoriously poor as instruments, lacking reliability and usually loaded on the bottom end of rote memorization test items requiring little, if any, upper-level thinking or problem-solving abilities on the part of the students. This situation often is reflective of the actual teaching situation, however, which is concentrated upon rote work in the great bulk of teaching time (see Lien, 1976, pp. 25–51; Yeh, 2001).

In other cases, the local instructional program is far too complex and complicated to be used as the base to apply traditional standardized measures. A key example is that students in language experience or "whole language"-based programs, which are increasing in popularity, often fare poorly on traditional standardized tests of language acquisition, which are based on traditional reading approaches dominant in most reading textbooks. So, one of the problems with frontloading as a practice is the lack of appropriate measures for determining success when the program is radically different than those upon which standardized tests are aligned.

B. The Bogeyman of "Teaching to the Test"

The practice of frontloading universally establishes that "teaching to the test" occurs. If a local educator writes a local curriculum and then develops a local test to assess whether or not children have learned that local curriculum—when teachers teach to the local curriculum—they are also "teaching to the local test." If the curriculum and the test are virtually the same, *teaching to the test is inevitable and desired.* In fact, the extent to which any test is useful in reteaching any given curriculum is the extent to which that test does indeed measure the curriculum in the first place.

If the test provides data about some curriculum other than the one developed locally, the information may be interesting, but it isn't useful in improving teaching or learning because it has little to do with what that teaching or learning is about, that is, as it pertains to the actual content of both processes. This is one reason that much of what data are produced by standardized tests isn't used at local levels. The fact is that the data may have little do to with the actual curriculum in place at the local level.

C. Critical Assumptions of Randomness Violated

The makers of standardized tests desire a low alignment to any purely local curriculum (which means the test content doesn't match the local curriculum content directly). This has to be true, or it would be possible for some districts to do much better than others simply based on the fact that some alignments were much better than others.

This situation would violate a critical assumption regarding randomness that all makers of standardized test instruments must assume. Randomness means that test scores can only be compared if all children who take the test have the same chance of learning that which it measures. Put another way, "This curve is often called a *normal* distribution curve because it approximates distribution according to the mathematical laws of probability or chance" (Lincoln, 1924, p. 33). If this were not so, some children would score better simply because of their circumstances, which in turn violates the principle of randomness or chance.

Early test makers assumed that it was possible to assess intelligence independently of the environment (Samuda, 1975, p. 63). This assumption is *false* because socioeconomic status does predict what a student's score will be on a standardized test, far more so than the school's curricula or its size (with an assumed low alignment to the local curriculum; see Fowler & Walberg, 1991). International data show that the importance of socioeconomic background is related to student test performance more in some countries than others. For example, in criticizing the failure of schools in Germany, *The Economist* (2006) noted that, "a 15-year-old's school record depended more heavily on socioeconomic background than other big industrial countries" (p. 7). Other countries that also showed a relationship were the United States, France, Sweden, and Poland.

This means that *wealth* predicts a student's score, and *wealth* is not a random variable in the larger society. Or in the words of researcher Christopher Jencks (1972, p. 53), "Variations in what children learn in school depend largely on variations in what they bring to school, not on variations in what schools offer them." The fact that environmental factors such as socioeconomic status and the amount of schooling and language influenced test scores was postulated in 1935 by Klineberg.

Some psychometricians postulate that teaching anything about the test, its format or content, directly is an unethical practice (Haladyna, Nolen, & Haas, 1991). They posit that test items are drawn from a potential "bank" of items that are purported to assess a "construct of achievement." If one teaches to specific items, a pupil may look good but not actually understand the larger "construct," and so his or her score may be fallacious. The function of this argument is to deny to local educators any prior knowledge of what a test assesses, thus ensuring a random distribution of scores and a bell-shaped curve, the so-called normal distribution of scores.

This interstitial idea between what tests measure and the use of tests in making judgments about schools, teachers, and curricula is the logical link between the continued use of such tests and the capability of applying them to make judgments about the quality of that application locally. The so-called construct of achievement concept, if taken to the extreme advocated by some test purists, simply results in allowing race, gender, and wealth to continue to predict test scores and enables those with a strong eugenics bias in social policy construction explaining them to continue their misuse of statistical information (see House & Haug, 1995; Lincoln, 1997). For a review of the original assumptions regarding how the bell curve or normal distribution was first created and became the basis of the eugenics movement, see Kevles (1999, pp. 13–19)

D. Textbooks as Curricula Affect Alignment and Test Scores

Of course, local textbook adoption and the varying rates of alignment to known standardized tests shed new light on the impact of in-school factors. Leaving that fact aside for the moment, how then are such test data useful in improving the delivery of a purely local curriculum if they don't match that curriculum?

The answer is that low alignments to local curriculum cast serious doubts on the efficacy of standardized tests in really assessing what any local school or school system is attempting to do in the first place. The comparisons are not made to the local curriculum but to the place of other students who are also pursuing a vastly different curriculum or at least a curriculum whose similarity to any other local curriculum is unknown. Students can't be compared on content mastery because no claim can be made about content similarity from one site to the next or from one state to the next. All that can be said is that information from standardized tests shows how one student is doing compared with another student on an assumed or *mythical national curriculum* that is unspecified in the name of assessing the construct of achievement.

The great weakness of standardized tests in providing useful information to local classroom teachers and administrators is that the data they provide are practically of no use unless the alignment (match) with the local curriculum is known (see Resnick & Resnick, 1985, p. 12). When that becomes known, test data have a great deal of relevance to local educators and then become *feedback.* Feedback occurs when the data regarding the actual learning of students can be attached in concrete ways to what teachers are supposed to (and ultimately do) teach their students.

Frontloading as a practice preserves the idea of local control of the curriculum, although with increasing reliance on standardized and statewide criterion-referenced tests (not to mention the historical reliance on textbooks, which have exercised a profound "standardizing impact" on the taught curriculum), such control is fast fading as a reality on the U.S. educational scene. What remains of local control is primarily about the politics of taxation and in many places school boundaries. Except for occasional "spats" over evolution and sex education, curricular issues are rarely the stuff of heated controversy in most local school systems.

E. Disadvantages of Frontloading as a Curriculum Practice

The disadvantages of using frontloading as a dominant practice in the development of curriculum are that (a) no curriculum can ever be considered a purely localized product given the mobility of students and their families in the United States and (b) it takes an excessive amount of time to develop a curriculum prior to the time local educators may have the option of selecting a test that "matches" that local curriculum. As a by-product of the second problem, frontloading is the most expensive way to obtain alignment because an entire curriculum has to be written before it can be aligned. However, even as school system personnel move to consider backloading as a more practical and immediate response to the strictures of high-stakes testing, at some point some frontloading will have to occur principally because tests are always measures of "what is" and not "what should be." They are measures of the past and not the future. To come to terms with what "should be" in schools beyond tests, a curriculum will have to be created even if only in the barest and crudest of forms. Also, most state's curricula represents not the highest and most demanding set of standards, but only the minimal set of expectations for the largest number of school districts in that state. In that situation to use the state's curriculum as the "final" or "best" measure of curricular rigor would be nothing but a chimera.

F. "Bubble-Up" Curriculum Practices in Schools

Local curriculum practice in most school districts is dominated by a process that could be called "the bubble-up model of curriculum development." Essentially, this practice begins when groups of teacher are commissioned to "write" curriculum, usually in the summer. Such groups are rarely provided guidelines or formats or even information on basic concepts such as alignment or tightening.

What often emerges from such projects is a vague set of platitudes and cookbook-type lessons that are unrelated, that are incoherent in terms of overall focus, and that remain unevaluated or assessed.

"Bubble-up" curriculum models make a fuss about process but produce products that are unusable even by those who created them in the first place. Often, they are so ambiguous that test alignment is nearly impossible to attain because test item content is much more specific, and hence dominates the alignment process, and by default becomes a form of *backloading* instead of frontloading.

Although nearly all curriculum textbooks at the university level advocate a form of frontloading, when found in local school districts, the process is so undefined and open ended that the work plans produced by it are rarely "user friendly" and have little impact on what teachers do in actual classrooms when supervisors or administrators are not around. The primary weaknesses of frontloading are that it is expensive and unproductive. Teachers are reluctant to write very specific plans for fear that, as work-related documents, they may in turn be evaluated by the system officials using them to ensure conformance. Such work documents are kept quite general and open ended to protect teachers against this form of work control and potentially heavy-handed evaluative practices.

This is the real agenda in frontloading curriculum because it revolves around defining the work to be done without also providing the means to enable closer supervision and evaluation from occurring simultaneously (see Dreeben, 1973). These two forces are contradictory and produce a tension that is usually never addressed and is left unresolved in local curriculum development practices. For this reason, teacher developed curriculum will usually leave space for them to work and to avoid excessively "tight" conformance.

Simultaneously, such space also leaves room for multiple interpretations of curriculum content, which similarly leaves open the potential "surprise situation" for students who were not adequately prepared for the test to which they must pass. This issue of conformance, clarity, and control is not only contentious but also not well understood in its many manifestations. If approached purely as a rational and technical issue in securing a "tight" fit between the written and taught curricula, is not likely to be resolved to anyone's satisfaction, for example, curriculum leaders and classroom teachers.

G. When Frontloading Is Impossible or Is Not Likely to Bring the Desired Results

As a practice, frontloading is impossible whenever local educators must use a mandated test with an unknown match to its local curriculum. In this circumstance, frontloading only really works when local educators design their own curriculum and select their own test. If this is not possible, frontloading is not possible, especially if the tests are of the high-stakes variety. The only real decision to be made is whether to backload or not. Of course, if all local control is forfeited and what is "local" is simply the state's curriculum imposed on local schools, then the major concern shifts to the extent to which the state's curriculum is adequately reflected and aligned with the state's test. The evidence of good alignment between them has not been overwhelming so far (see Webb, 1997,1999, 2002). There are a variety of reasons for this, not the least of which is any state's method for developing its curriculum and whether it writes its own test or lets it be contracted out to a "for profit" company.

3.2 THE PROCESS OF ALIGNMENT VIA BACKLOADING

Alignment refers to the "match" between the curriculum's content, context, and cognitive levels to be taught and the test content to be used in assessing pupil learning. *Backloading* refers to the practice of establishing the match by working from the test "back to" the curriculum. It means that the test *becomes the curriculum*. In this case, there is always 100% alignment because the curriculum to be taught was derived from the test to be administered. However, whatever imperfections, errors, or biases are present in the test are also reflected in the curriculum since the latter is the former.

A. Implications of Backloading as a Practice

There are at least two implications for *backloading*. The first is that whoever wrote the test wrote the curriculum and unless the test constructors were also local, local control is thus sacrificed. Test writers, especially those who were paid by testing companies to write test items, represent a small elite of individuals who define in concrete terms what was actually meant by curriculum writers who wrote ambiguous curriculum frameworks. This "space" is notorious as a disconnect between a frontloaded, a priori curriculum, and a backloaded after the fact, and it doesn't matter what they desired curriculum. Test developers work in a different space than curriculum developers. Test developers have to be acutely aware of a variety of forms of ambiguity in writing clear test items. If the curriculum is unclear, there is a lot of room for guessing what was meant. The space in which this occurs promotes very wide ranges of variance for local practitioners. Whereas they can interpret ambiguous curriculum content one way, test developers may see it quite differently. The test, however, is the ultimate arbiter in confronting curricular ambiguity.

The second is that the issue of "teaching to the test" is raised as a possible source of unethical or unwise procedure.

The first issue of "local control" has already been addressed. One way to assess what may be lost by backloading is to examine the test itself (if possible) and determine whether there is anything on the instrument one believes ought not to be taught to students and thus tested. If the answer is negative, it matters little what the test is assessing because learners would have been taught what is present regardless.

Another check is more profound. A local educator may ask, "Is there anything that a local student should know that this test isn't assessing?" To answer that question, some frontloading has to occur because it assumes that the content of the curriculum is in some way knowable or known. How else would the question be answered? A purely *backloaded* curriculum would not ask the question, which concerns the "null curriculum," that is, the content not included in a curriculum. The act of "nonselection" is value laden, and in this case, the values nonselected by the test makers represent an unknown element that may be at odds with local values.

B. The Issue of "Teaching to the Test"

The issue of "teaching to the test" remains one of the most nettlesome problems in the whole alignment process. Some researchers have called the idea of *alignment*—that is, matching the test and curriculum content—"unethical" (see Haladyna, Nolen, & Haas, 1991, p. 4).

What is unethical about the practice is that test makers desired a kind of response called the "normal curve," a frequency distribution of scores that looks like the bell shape in Figure 3.2.

To derive this shape, several assumptions are made about the scores. The first is that the property or variable being assessed exists in the larger population more or less like height or weight (see Kevles, 1999, pp. 13–19; Mehrens & Lehmann, 1987, p. 41). This is a very debatable assumption. Nonetheless, to attain the "normal curve" in assessing learner outcomes, further assumptions have to be made regarding whether or not all the children start at the same point and/or that factors outside purely "learning" are not at work skewing the "normal" curve positively or negatively. It has been noted already that socioeconomic level definitely skews learner outcomes, which do not assume a normal curve if large

Figure 3.2   The Bell-Shaped Curve

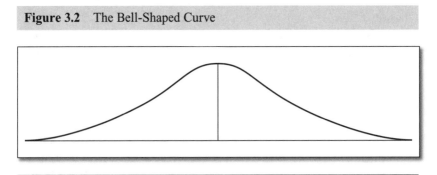

NOTE: To arrive at a frequency distribution in the form of a bell-shaped curve, randomness or chance must be functional in order to get a continuous distribution of responses resembling this form. Yet schools, teachers, administration, and curriculum cannot be considered "random" acts or "chance" variables. Test secrecy does not permit alignment, and so school-related variables may appear random when they are not.

populations of learners from lower socioeconomic groups are included in a sample. So the act of comparison at the outset is specious unless the comparisons are explained.

For a normal curve to be desired as a frequency distribution, it has to be assumed that there is only a tangential relationship between the test and the curriculum (low alignment). If the alignment were not low, then those groups that engaged a curriculum with a higher match would do better on the test. If the alignment were quite high, there would be nothing wrong with teaching to the test because it wouldn't result in improved test scores.

Behind the quality of low alignment is the *assumption of randomness,* because whatever is being measured on a test is assumed to be a *continuous variable* (like height or weight). Anything else would not produce a normal distribution (see Kevles, 1999, pp. 13–19; Popham, 1981, p. 159; White, 2006). If alignment occurs, then some persons or groups would score better than they would have had they not had access to this "match." The score distribution then becomes discontinuous or nonrandom as a result, producing a skewed or irregular distribution.

Another word for *random* is *chance.* Chance is the *critical* assumption that is absolutely essential in test theory (see Magnusson, 1966, pp. 4–8). It means that if groups of students are going to be compared on some similar and assumed continuous variable, all should have not only the same opportunity to be selected in the sample but also the same exposure to the variable being assessed, and furthermore, all should respond more or less in the same fashion (see Bertrand & Cebula, 1980, p. 116).

If this were not so, some members would skew the distribution or frequency of scores whatever way their exposure matched or did not match the assessment tool or process. External factors to the school already skew student response on tests, which results in a noncontinuous distribution or nonrandom distribution.

Another problem lies in using test scores to compare students, teachers, administrators, and curriculum and/or programs, one to the other, based on such data. For such comparisons to be valid, one or more assumptions have to be made. All of them are specious (see Mehrens & Lehmann, 1987, p. 194).

The first assumption that has to be made is that the "treatments" received by the students in the first place were themselves continuous or random; that is, they assumed the properties of a normal distribution. This must be so—for comparisons between students and, by inference, teachers, administrators, and curriculum and/or programs cannot be made. School itself has to be considered a random variable to result in the distribution of scores based on the idea of a continuous variable.

Yet, in reality, no school is a random variable. All schools are nonrandom, that is, *purposive places* where activities are goal directed. Administrators, teachers, and curricula are nonrandom variables as well. If judgments are going to be made about the quality or effectiveness of teachers, administrators, curricula, or programs on the basis of a test score, then it has to be conceded that they are *purposive variables and nonrandom by design* or schools cannot be accountable for what they do.

It has to be assumed that if schools did something differently than they were doing before (a nonrandom act), then their actions would not result in the production of a continuous variable and a normal curve. A normal curve assumes that 50% of the population must be below average for the assumption regarding a continuous variable to hold.

Inasmuch as test scores are driven largely by socioeconomic factors, schools that serve large populations of lower-socioeconomic students are automatically assigned to the "below average" category. This is *social determinism* based on wealth. It doesn't matter what teachers or administrators do in developing a curriculum or reforming programs; they will automatically be "worse" based on the students they serve. In the words of one Ohio legislator who viewed the test results of the first statewide exam, "We spent a million and a half dollars to find out that poor kids did worse than rich ones." The achievement test results closely match socioeconomic level in most states and regions around the United States (see Sax, 1980, pp. 373–379) and continue to show differences in scores by race that is connected to measures of wealth (Tomsho, 2009).

"Teaching to the test" is an issue with the test makers because it tampers with the idea of test results being considered a continuous variable. If some students are taught what they are tested on, they will obviously do better than if they were not so instructed. Thus, what is assumed to be a continuous variable becomes skewed or discontinuous. Teaching to the test jams the bell-shaped curve! It produces a "J" curve, which means that the scores are all above average. The distribution is positively skewed, as shown in Figure 3.3.

The classic problem in teaching to the test is that students are learning only the test item and not the concept, process, or idea that

Figure 3.3 The "J" Curve

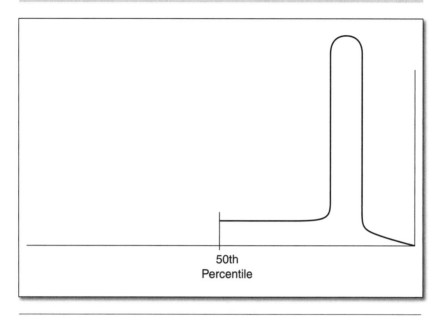

50th
Percentile

NOTE: The "J" occurs when all children are learning and "above average." Curriculum-test alignment at both the content and the context levels is one way to approach the "J" curve.

lies behind it (Cronbach, 1963, p. 681). So, if they score well on a test, the scores don't necessarily represent what they really know or don't know. "Teaching to the test is therefore viewed by some as a kind of 'pollution' of the 'true meaning' of what a score might indicate if this condition were not present. One of the controversies surrounding test score 'pollution' is that connected with the test prep industry and the SAT. Test prep companies like Kaplan and the Princeton Review and others often make claims about score improvement. They have developed tests which mirror that of the SAT itself, a classic case of alignment in matching test content, context and level of cognition. The objection to such a practice is that a report by the National Association for College Admission Counseling 'finds fault with the frequent use of mock SAT tests because they can be devised to inflate score gains when students take the actual SAT'" (Hechinger, 2009a, p. D1). So the objection is that there would be a different distribution of scores without this nonrandom interference and that inferences from whatever the SAT is assessing from a larger content domain would be jeopardized.

Such an assertion also rests on an assumption that in some way the curricula all students would take did not contain enough variance to also cause a lack of fairness in the results when such inequities abound already at the socioeconomic level and with race (see Sacks, 1997). The advantages of wealth in improving access to higher education also represent a nonrandom "interference" in the population to be sampled.

Besides, this report shows that so-called "coaching" (a form of alignment) only raises the average SAT score by 30 points. But this gain may be significant because some colleges have indicated that a gain of just 20 points in the math part of the SAT and 10 points in the critical reading part would "significantly improve students' likelihood of admission" (Hechinger, 2009a, p. D7).

The major problem with this assertion is that test scores must assume the property of a continuous variable producing a bell curve to be considered rigorous, and alignment produces a nonrandom distribution of scores.

The most common form of a nonrandom test response occurs on the weekly spelling test so pervasive in the nation's elementary school classrooms. That procedure begins with the teacher introducing 25 words on Monday, the class studying those words through Wednesday—when a practice test is provided on the same 25 words—followed on Friday by a test that again measures the same 25 words. The classroom teacher does not sample these words. He or she does not resort to "Form B" of a test so that the words are unfamiliar to the students.

What is desired is a nonrandom response on the part of the class. Most teachers hope that all students will earn 100% and spell the 25 words!

If the teacher wanted a random distribution, he or she would not have taught the students at all about the 25 words. If one desires 50% of the class to be below average, the best way to ensure that this is the result is to avoid teaching students that which you intend to test them on because *teaching will make such a difference.*

Teaching will produce a nonrandom or non-normal distribution, particularly if it matches the test. If one is not teaching what one is testing, how can judgments be made about the quality of teaching based on a test score? If a test does not match a school's curriculum, how can test scores be used as a measure of the quality of the curriculum?

Because tests do measure acquired behavior and learning, if that learning has not been acquired in school, it has to have been acquired somewhere. The answer is that it is acquired in the larger socioeconomic arena, which is why socioeconomic level plays such a large role in predicting test results. Students taking tests with low alignments are largely bounded by the lessons learned (or not learned) in their socioeconomic level.

Socioeconomic determinism is the consequence of using standardized norm-referenced tests, which pretend to be "objective" measures of pupil learning when they are anything but "objective." If such tests were truly objective, there would be no predictor variables that could account for their frequency except truly random cases. Wealth is not the same property as height and weight. And in no case should school or school-related factors such as teaching, administration, or curriculum development be considered random variables.

But a test with a low alignment to a school's teaching or curriculum makes it appear as if factors were random because none of them predicts the scores (because there is scant or no connection between what is going on in classrooms and the extent to which any kind of measurement is aligned). Low test-curriculum alignment makes it appear as if schooling were a continuous, random variable. If schooling truly were such a random variable, then all of the purposive activities in a school that direct and focus teaching would be fixed ahead of time by the communities in which they happen to be located and their socioeconomic conditions.

If, then, tests are to be used to assess pupil learning, quality teaching, sound administration, and productive curriculum, they have to have a planned overlap to what these activities are about. When that overlap is planned so that what one measures is what one wants to occur, *alignment is present and the measurement does not produce a normal curve.* The frequency distribution will resemble a much more positively skewed result than the bell-shaped template so familiar in testing circles.

Comparison of students, teachers, administrators, curricula, programs, and the like must be made on the basis of a test tightly aligned to their activities, or (a) the scores cannot be considered valid indicators of the activities and (b) scores cannot be compared validly in terms of doing anything about them to improve subsequent outcomes.

The major problem with the bell curve is that it is precisely the wrong distribution of scores to assess *purposive behavior that is essentially nonrandom by design, which is the essence of schooling*! Ralph Tyler (1974) noted that achievement testing in World War I was strongly linked to intelligence testing, which assumed a normal curve. Says Tyler (1974, p. 147), "Actually, school programs are based on contrary assumptions." Continuous warnings against "teaching to the test" allow nonschool variables to dominate and predict test scores rather than in-school variables predicting them. It dooms schools and school systems serving lower socioeconomic children always to being labeled "poor schools" when what they should properly be labeled is "schools serving the poor." The answer is that schools should test what they teach and teach what they test.

C. Dealing With Unethical Applications of Standardized Tests

To be used properly, standardized tests assume that all in-school variables can be factored in such a way that they can be "random," and if influential, take on the characteristics of a continuous variable. If this were not so, the bell-shaped curve could not be considered the proper "form" in displaying the scores obtained on the test norms. To control for possible bias in the sample of respondents constituting the norm, great care has to be taken in selecting those included. If mostly Quakers were somehow part of a test group and a question about war were asked, the preponderance of pacifists would provide a very different distribution than one in which Quakers were not a majority.

If all of the school districts in a state that intended to use some sort of state standardized test were assessed on an assumed random variable, the distribution of scores would be expected to resemble a bell curve. By definition, on any characteristic, 50% of the school districts are expected to be "below average." If a state makes no move to punish those school districts on the bottom (who are more than likely to be poor in terms of extant socioeconomic variables), then the test simply reflects the bias in the various communities in which the schools function. "Teaching to the test" may change the distribution, but if no judgments are being made about the quality of teaching—curriculum, administration, and the like—it doesn't really matter what the score is.

If the state, its agents, or other public persons are going to punish the school district, its schools, teachers, or administrators based on a test score, then the results of the test have been unethically applied (see Cangelosi, 1991, p. 105).

First, the bell-shaped curve *requires* a 50% failure rate, and no distribution would be accepted as accurate unless this were the case. Second, teaching, curriculum development, and administration are not random acts but purposive, goal-directed ones. Change the goal of teaching to include more of the content of the test, and the scores will improve on the same test. Tests cannot be used to assess these characteristics if they don't match up with what is being taught. The whole assumption of purposiveness requires alignment to be present. Otherwise, the data are useless in terms of trying to improve because there is no fit to what is being assessed. Furthermore, if teachers, students, and administrators can't improve with subsequent tests, how can the data be used to measure their effectiveness? In other words, if test data acquisition has no "effects," what is the value of having the test in the first place?

It is unethical to "teach to a test" if the purpose of the test is truly to assess a random variable that is assumed to contain the characteristics of a continuous variable within the population being assessed. In this scenario, it would be imprudent to make judgments that at the base *assume* that characteristics indirectly connected to the variable (quality of teaching, administration, curriculum development) being directly assessed (for example, a student achievement score in math) are essentially continuous as well.

Once such an indirect variable is affected by changes derived from a test score, it ceases to be random even if it were so considered initially. Thus, the logic of standardized tests breaks down when moving from direct assessment of the assumed psychological properties of students (learning) to those factors that are supposed to be important in producing the effects but that are noncontinuous and nonrandom in nature. Sooner or later, those indirect factors cease to be random.

That has to be the case if such variables are to be judged in some way as to effectiveness of performance. One cannot continually blame teachers for poor test scores if their behavior has no impact on learning. So teaching has to be envisioned as a purposive, nonrandom, noncontinuous activity that does not assume the properties of a bell-shaped curve (see Smith, 1991; Smith & Rottenberg, 1991).

The norm of assessment in most other human activities, from manufacturing to athletics, is that one always teaches to the test. The basketball coach would never be told by the principal, "Your team may not practice, that would be cheating! Furthermore, you may not scout the other team or obtain films of the other team. You may not know what offense or defense they plan to run at your team. That would all be cheating! Just get your team ready to play by telling them, 'Don't think about the game at all. When the time comes, just do the best you can!'"

No basketball coach would accept these conditions in a competitive basketball league. But we tell classroom teachers virtually the same thing all the time when it comes to "practicing for the achievement test."

No manufacturer would use an assessment instrument to measure worker performance that wasn't indexed to the product being turned out and its quality. Worker performance is only relative to the product and its quality. And no manufacturer wants a bell curve! That would mean 50% of the products would be rejects. So the assessment of manufacturing goods is indexed (aligned) to the product being produced. Worker performance is directly keyed to the product. Measurement criteria are indexed to the product so that they match. Otherwise, using "feedback" would not be very useful in improving the product with subsequent applications in production.

It is this fact that lies at the heart of the statement that the bell-shaped curve is an inappropriate distribution to assess the quality of schools, the teaching in them, or the quality of the curriculum being used by teachers in their work. So what is unethical behavior?

If, on the other hand, the curriculum and the test are matched (aligned) and everyone knows what the alignment is, then the quality of teaching, of curriculum, and of administration can be assessed and directed, because the fact of "no surprises" for the students has been ruled out as a *causative factor* in explaining the differences between the scores. The determinism of socioeconomic level is decreased as a predictor. The school now becomes *the* qualitative factor in explaining pupil achievement because achievement scores are directly related to what happens in them.

In sports, if every team scouts every other team, practices against their preferred offense and defense, then the quality of their preparation and practice and their motivation and conditioning become the determiners of the results. It is highly unlikely that these characteristics assume the form of a bell-shaped curve. They are much more likely to be a "J" curve, clustered near the positive end of the curve producing a tight skew. "J" curves have been called by Allport in 1932 (as cited in Guilford, 1936) measures of "institutional behavior."

Local educators in some states are continually confronted with a scenario in which the state education agency is going to test all the children in the state but actually desires a 50% failure rate embodied in a bell curve. The only way that such a distribution can occur is to keep the test a secret, which ensures randomness because it means that the content, the format, and the procedures contained in the test are unknown to everyone.

In this procedure, the purposiveness (nonrandomness) of the school has been negated by excluding the test content from the curriculum and from the teaching practices. The school, therefore, can be statistically treated as a random variable producing a continuous variable. However debatable this procedure may be, logically no judgments can be made about the quality of schools because those variables that are purposive (teaching, curriculum, grouping, and so on) have been reduced to random (nonpurposiveness) variables by keeping the test a secret and ensuring a low alignment of the test content with the curriculum content.

In such a scenario, the impact of the curriculum is negligible. This was demonstrated by the Coleman study of 1966 in which standardized achievement tests were used to probe for school-related variables that would have an effect upon pupil achievement. That study noted, "differences between schools account for only a small fraction of differences in pupil achievement" (Coleman, 1966, p. 22). The assumption upon which such differences rest is that "schools are remarkably similar in the way they relate to the achievement of their pupils" (p. 21).

What has happened here is that, by forcing a low content-content alignment from test to curriculum, in-school variables that could make a difference are blunted and don't make a difference. This undergirds the argument that schools are random (or all alike), in which case they become random by using random inclusion procedures. The result is a bell-shaped curve when pupil characteristics—their race and socioeconomic status—form the base for the distribution of scores as opposed to any in-school purposive (nonrandom) variable such as curriculum or facilities.

D. What Is Cheating on Tests?

Psychometric purists would define *cheating* as teaching anything remotely concerned with a test. It has been shown that their loyalty is given to assumptions regarding randomness and the necessity to base their predictions on a normal curve of the distribution of scores centered on ideas behind intelligence testing (see Jensen, 1980, pp. 71–74). Intelligence is assumed to be a characteristic like height or weight in the overall population and was named "general intelligence" so that tests could assess it similarly (see Terman, 1916, pp. 36–50; White, 2006). Results from using the Binet test in America were assumed to be biological rather than cultural even though Binet himself did not envision intelligence as biological (see Marks, 1981, pp. 18–19). Any "tampering" with test items believed to be biological (as opposed to cultural) that would not result in obtaining a normal distribution would be considered a violation of some underlying (and hence "true") "natural" condition.

That this is *the assumption* is shown by the analogy of some psychometricians to teaching someone to read a Snellen eye chart and then, when attaining a better score, attributing the gain to "better" eyes (Mehrens & Kaminski, 1988). If one expects to find a normal distribution based on biology, then any attempt to alter that distribution would be prohibited. Psychometricians who believe in "genetic predeterminism" may call any such intrusions "pollution" or "unethical practices" (see White, 2006).

As we have seen, however, there is a considerable body of professional opinion that the bell curve is inappropriate in assessing pupil achievement related to classroom teaching and purposive (nonrandom) behavior patterns. Philip Morrison (1977, p. 89), a physics professor at the Massachusetts Institute of Technology, has written, "I am disturbed that the sophisticates of educational statistics have written so little about the other distributions [those other than the bell-shaped curve] . . . . Until they have done so, I rest fearful that they have mistaken mere consistency for observation, and a circle for a clear line of argument." What Morrison means is that the results of such tests should not be used to rate teachers, schools, or curricula because these factors are not distributed randomly in the population to be sampled, even though statistical assumptions and attendant secrecy result in reinforcing the belief that they are random and nonpurposive.

In reality, schools, teachers, and curricula cannot be random variables assuming the dimensions of a bell or Gaussian (for the mathematician Karl Gauss) curve. If they were, the whole idea of *accountability* would be absurd, and the purpose of such tests is to *establish accountability.* This basic logical incompatibility between biologically determined test norms and engaging in judgments about the quality of schools, teachers, principals, and curricula has led some to call for a moratorium on all standardized testing (Fine, 1975, p. 140).

Cheating on tests may be construed as allowing students to see or practice with the actual test itself prior to its administration, providing students with more time than is allotted to complete their answers, assisting students to solve test items during the test, or changing student answers after the test has been taken.

3.3 HOW TO DO ALIGNMENT

We have now seen how alignment can work from a frontloading perspective or from the view of backloading. The most common form of frontloading occurs in the textbook adoption cycle. If alignment is part of the criteria by which textbooks as work plans are adopted, then the books with the highest alignment should be adopted. Figure 3.4 shows this process.

Figure 3.4 shows the adoption of a textbook based on the test (a backload). In frontloading, the textbook with the maximum match to the local curricular outcomes would be adopted. Suppose that a text is adopted that produces a 40% match to the local curricular outcomes. Then local curriculum development would be required to complete the remaining 60%. The same figures would hold on a backload if the test is what is being matched to the textbook.

Figure 3.4   Preliminary Alignment Practices

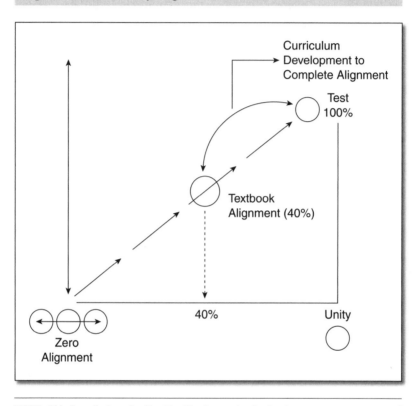

NOTE: This is a display of a "backload" using textbook adoption to test as a measure of alignment. Curriculum development is then employed to complete the alignment.

A. Determine the Context in Which Alignment Will Occur

How a school or school district approaches the alignment issue must be largely determined by the context in which the process is to occur. Propriety of alignment, and whether one should *frontload* or *backload,* is set by the contextual scenario surrounding the alignment issue.

If a school or school system is facing an externally imposed testing program in which the test makers desire a bell-shaped curve (a 50% failure rate) and negative consequences accrue to the school or the school system after the test has been administered, then the situation is one in which local officials should seriously consider backloading. This may be difficult given the climate of secrecy that often prevails when states or other external agencies desire to assess schools or school districts on test items that if exposed publicly, would allow learning to occur, thus skewing the results more positively than is desired. (It may be observed that nothing messes up a bell curve more than pupil learning!)

School district teachers and officials have to watch carefully that their actions are not labeled "teaching to the test" when they take steps to backload. The "ethics" of testing often prohibit backloading in any form except a very general one, and context alignment is usually forbidden.

There are at least two levels of alignment. The first is *content alignment* in which the content of the test is matched to the content of the curriculum. The second level is *context alignment,* sometimes called *format alignment,* in which the shape of the assessment item is taught as well as the content of the item.

Thus, if spelling is to be tested, the way it is tested is as important as the words to be assessed. Typically, standardized tests use a form of word recognition as the method for assessing spelling. Spelling, however, is usually taught as direct recall of the way a word is derived from sounds provided orally by the teacher. One may be able to recognize a correct word when given but be unable to reproduce it from scratch when oral cues alone are provided.

Makers of standardized tests sometimes balk at providing format examples of test items, even though, with such nationally standardized tests as the Graduate Record Exam, examples may be purchased in book form prior to taking the test. Format or context alignment is an important variable in any testing scenario. Providing information about format is helpful in preparing students to take tests. If this were not so, most graduate students would not be asking their instructors if the final exam will be true/false, multiple choice, or essay in nature.

Any athletic coach will want to know what offense or defense an opponent will run so as to prepare his or her team to recognize these forms and respond accordingly. In football, the whole concept of "audibles"—that is, changes of play calling at the line of scrimmage—is based on the recognition of the "format" facing the offensive team.

Alignment is a very old concept in education. Much of the theory behind it was developed by Thorndike (1913) in his creation of the "identical theory of the transfer of training" and later expanded to the transfer by *generalization*. What this idea means is that, "unless the new situation has enough in common with the previous one for the learner to perceive applications, no transfer occurs" (Klausmeier & Goodwin, 1966, p. 473).

Alignment is facilitated when situations are taught so that the learner more readily recognizes them when they occur. It would be like a quarterback learning to read the defenses of the opponent quickly enough to call audibles. The quarterback must be able to "transfer" the knowledge of which play works best against which defense by moving from one situation (a play called in anticipation of a set defense) to a different play (when the situation encountered was not the one anticipated). *Transfer* is facilitated when the situations are similar and recognizable by the learner. *Alignment* is a process of teaching the learner to recognize similar situations (content and formats) by which assessment will take place.

In situations where test results are very negatively applied and poor scores trigger even more undesirable consequences like inspections, sanctions, or takeover possibilities, local school officials should consider backloading from tests to localized work plans that teachers follow in the form of simple checklists to teach specific content, examples of formats, or specially developed curricula that include both.

Care must be taken so as to operate within state-defined limitations of test-curriculum matchups. If these are prohibitive, district or school officials may wish to take on officials or regulations that operate on the assumption that scores must follow the laws of "natural" determinism where results form a continuous variable in a bell-shaped curve. Officials may obtain data from the state showing that socioeconomic variables are the strongest predictors of pupil performance, and not school-related ones. The "genetic" basis of the bell curve is much more culturally produced than the policymakers will find comfortable.

The "tightness" of the fit between backloading from the test, shaping teaching to ensure alignment, and curriculum construction is shaped by the requirements of the situation. "Tightening" occurs when the children involved are nearly dependent upon the school as the only avenue open to them to perform well on the tests. The schools cannot depend upon the socioeconomic level of their community to hold up their test scores because it is already quite low. The only means to improve a test score is to teach that which the test will measure and to do it as well as the situation permits.

B. Determine the Most
Efficacious Form of Backloading

The form backloading takes is contingent upon (a) how much time the school or system has to improve test scores, (b) the resources at the school or system's disposal, (c) the nature of the pupils and teachers involved, (d) the complexities of the test itself, and (e) the extent of the alignment extant in existing textbooks and other forms of school materials in use.

If the school or the system has very little time in which to improve test scores before sanctions are applied, the creation of simple checklists geared to the test is probably the most efficacious form of backloading. The second step is to make sure teachers know how to perform the content and skills, procedures, and protocols required by the test so that their classroom teaching includes all of these areas. Staff development becomes a crucial ingredient of any successful backloading program.

It ought to be mentioned that the purchase of sophisticated hardware packages, learning laboratories, computers, and the like will not improve alignment unless it is specifically determined prior to any such purchase. There is nothing "magical" about hardware and labs unless the curriculum of the test and the content of the computers are aligned. Such materials may be no more aligned than the simple purchase of textbooks would ensure.

C. After Backloading, Determine Results and Gains

The efficacy of backloading is very limited and confined to the test itself. How much gain was recorded? Using the computer printouts from the test, perform an item analysis. Pinpoint where pupil responses were disappointing.

D. Locate Curricular Breakdowns in Extant Work Plans

To use test results to improve measured pupil performance, item analysis must be used to "link back" to whatever form of curriculum (or work plan) was being followed by classroom teachers. The "linking back" to the work plan is called "the reconnect." It means that test results are analyzed and reconnected or linked back to the work plans teachers were following. In this process, care is taken to ensure that changes are made in the work plans that will enhance measured pupil performance on future tests. This is the idea of *feedback*. An example would be a football team watching the films of the Saturday game on Monday to determine how best to improve their performance in subsequent practices and games. In fact, their gaps in performance *define the nature of practice*. The same idea would hold in the classroom.

E. Use Pareto Analysis to Correct the Important Errors

In analyzing mistakes, the Pareto Principle is usually followed; that is, the few account for the many (Burr, 1976, p. 203). The "few" in this case are deemed to be "fundamental errors," which will account for the greatest number of mistakes. This idea has been used with great effectiveness in the application of quality circles (Thompson, 1982, pp. 104–105) and is named after the great Italian economist and sociologist, Vilfredo Pareto (1848–1923; see Powers, 1987).

In reviewing test scores and items, for example, suppose that two or three errors account for nearly 53% of all errors. With the correction of these two or three, 53% of all errors may be corrected in subsequent performances. Instead of trying to correct every error, the Pareto Principle gives educational leaders the opportunity to select those that affect that greatest number of pupils, thus improving the size of the group doing better on subsequent tests. In statistics, the "n," or size of the number of persons in the sample, is a significant factor in improving measures of central tendency, that is, mean scores or group averages.

The principal or teacher leader will examine test results and select those that the largest number of students missed, looking for common patterns that unite them together. Once identified, these are "reconnected" to the work plan or curriculum and a revised set of instructions is provided for teachers to follow.

F. Construct Revised Work Plans Based on Pareto Analysis

This new set of directions based on Pareto analysis includes provisions for improved teaching of the tested concepts, skills, or content. Thus, by a continual iteration of working "back" from the test results, curriculum is more clearly focused on providing systematic instruction to pupils so that, with subsequent test iterations, their scores improve.

If the test is assessing complex problems that contain many skills, concepts, and knowledge, the "working back" to reconnect the test data to the curriculum (or textbooks) will stretch across more than one grade level. That means that the "correction" of the curriculum will involve multiple grades and more than one teacher over more than a year's period of time. Tracking back into a curriculum and redistributing the tested content may involve the development of "pacing charts." Such work plans involve the development of lessons over an extended time period that emphasize those areas in which alignment was poor or pupil performance was poor and concentrated teaching must occur in the designated areas. All tests are cumulative measures of pupil learning; that is, they assess not only what was taught at all grades before assessment but the "null" as well. The "null" represents what wasn't taught that should have been taught. Because tests are cumulative measures, where test scores indicate a problem is not necessarily where the problem is located or even corrected in the overall curriculum of a school or school system.

3.4 OTHER ISSUES IN THE ALIGNMENT PROCEDURE

Backloading to obtain alignment can produce very quick results in improved test scores (see Niedermeyer & Yelon, 1981, pp. 618–620). Written multiple-choice tests, however, are an inappropriate tool to assess many areas of desired learning that a sound curriculum may include.

Using tests as the source to develop curriculum runs the risk of accepting and defining learning only in terms of what can be assessed on a paper and pencil test within a multiple choice format. The means to assessment, and its inherent limitations, become the ends themselves and place a cap on the possibility of learning outside that which tests are assessing. That would be a tragedy of enormous proportions.

Backloading should be considered an interim measure to improve test scores and not as any kind of final answer to determining what should be in a curriculum in the first place. Considering what children should know is the quintessential problem facing the schools. That always involves the frontloading approach, and it should remain dominant despite the presence of increasing "high-stakes" testing and all of the negative consequences that accrue to students, teachers, and parents with their continued use.

CHAPTER FOUR

The Challenge of Curriculum Leadership in the Teaching and Testing Nexus

Most recently, an applicant for a middle school principalship in one school district wrote in his cover letter for a position in another district that in his past administrative experience he had helped his school make AYP (Adequate Yearly Progress) for the first time in seven years, increased end-of-grade math scores by 24.4 proficiency points, increased school end-of-grade reading scores by 16.2 proficiency points, and increased his school's composite score by 8.0 proficiency points. Exactly what do these numbers mean? What is happening to schools and the education in them when we reduce leadership responsibilities to such descriptors?

Do these "gains" mean this principal's school was a happy place where students were encouraged to learn and to explore things that peaked their curiosity? Did all students feel valued, or were some students demeaned or bored out of their minds in a test-prep factory environment? Were students' minds further closed to considering different issues or skills than those on the tests? Is this what some advocates mean by "data-driven decision making?" Is this all there is to becoming educated?

I am reminded here of the story of Enron that was once America's corporate darling, whose executives were called "the smartest guys in the room," and whose stock price was the envy of Wall Street. The mad pursuit of profit and the numbers, numbers, and numbers created a grim piranha culture that eclipsed any ethical or social responsibilities to its employees or the larger society. Enron resorted to a type of evaluation it called the PRC (Performance Review Committee) in which every employee was ranked against all others in the same business unit. The evaluations were done on a bell curve. The results could "account from 10% to as much as 26% of their total compensation" (Fox, 2003, p. 83). Employees who got ranked in the bottom 10% to 20% were cut from the payroll. The system was called by them the "rank and yank" plan. It resulted in excessive competition within the company and a ruthless quest for profits.

Enron executives created an artificial energy brownout in California that bilked the taxpayers of millions of dollars in the process of earning themselves huge bonuses. Enron was not just an example of one corporate bad apple. The culture of numbers irrespective of the larger ethical, moral, or social issues has infected many other organizations, public and private. Wal-Mart is another corporate monolith run by the numbers. The lawsuits brought against Wal-Mart by its former employees for cheating them out of overtime pay has resulted in some of the largest gender-based cash settlements in U.S. corporate history. In 2008, Wal-Mart agreed to pay up to $640 million to settle 63 lawsuits (Bustillo, 2008) Wal-Mart managers regularly manipulated their numbers so as not to report overtime or to erase it. Female employees were regularly expected (at the loss of their jobs) to put in hours for which they were not compensated. Wal-Mart also faced an unprecedented federal gender discrimination legal action that "is the largest class action lawsuit in U.S. history" (Bustillo, 2008, p. B1).

The number of corporate CEO's and CFO's indicted or in jail is testimony to the tyranny of managing by the numbers (Lauricella, 2004; Levitt & Breeden, 2003), and there is no reason not to believe that as school administrators become connected to such types of measures, similar scandals are just around the corner in education. The erosion of public service that first happened at university business schools (see Khurana, 2007) is now coming full force on education schools to shift their norms to business models in the mistaken belief that "for profit" perspectives will provide the incentive for needed reforms (see Anderson & Pini, 2005; Emery & Ohanian, 2004). The loss of a civic enterprise with a service orientation to a financial incentive model for test-score gains based on a competitive market model will lead to the whole-scale erosion of the values of growth and nurturance that undergird any healthy system of schools anywhere in the world (see Cuban, 2004). So when the phrase "data-driven decision making" is employed in the teaching-testing dyad, we should be prepared to ask, "Driven towards what?" and "Who ultimately benefits from such actions?"

When numbers become the ends in themselves, when "making the numbers" becomes what matters and not the activities that comprise them, we become captives to them and not their masters. They lead us around by the nose and distort and undermine a healthier and more inclusive perspective about not only education but also the role of schools in the larger society and what that society has become. What tests measure is the world as it is, warts and all, and not what it should or might become if a different set of values were embraced. Tests reinforce the social status quo, and to focus on them exclusively runs the risk of freezing the existing social order, injustices, inequities, exclusivities, and the prevailing power distribution of the here and now into the future. It is to this theme we now turn.

4.1 CONSIDERING THE FULL RESPONSIBILITY FOR CURRICULUM LEADERSHIP

To provide a measure of perspective regarding thinking about the nature of curriculum leadership today in the schools, we ought to briefly look back to a similar episode in the nation's educational history. The arguments and controversies surrounding accountability have been fought out before, so let's take a peek back to the last century to see what we might learn. This is the case of curriculum "activity analysis" advanced by Franklin Bobbitt (1918, 1971) a University of Chicago education professor who developed an approach to curriculum development that began not by philosophical deliberation, but by a practical approach of going into the larger society and analyzing the work tasks of people doing their jobs there. Bobbitt advanced his method by pointing out, "the curriculum discoverer will first be an analyst of human nature and human affairs . . . his first task . . . is to discover the total range of habits, skills, abilities, forms of thought, valuations, ambitions, and so on, that its members need for the effective performance of their vocational labors" (p. 43). We see a similar approach being advanced today by those who argue for minimal competency academic skills in mathematics, science, and language for the schools. The selection of such skill lists anchored in a broad array of consensual techniques from professional associations, subject area experts, think tank pundits, and editorial writers essentially freezes society at its current state in order to extrapolate them and also freezes the social hierarchy in which they function. As Bobbitt soon discovered, a school curriculum centered on "activity analysis" was soon obsolete. As one of his most powerful critics, Boyd Bode (1930) argued that Bobbitt's curriculum plan not only froze job roles in the larger social structure, it also froze the entire social structure with it along with the prevalent social practices of the times. Bode (1930) wrote, "An educational ideal that is content to train pupils for predetermined specific objectives is better suited to a static than to a dynamic social order" (p. 79). The same tensions exist today with predetermined educational objectives based on consensus lists from a variety of groups and interests. All of them represent a vested interest in maintaining the social status quo.

The teaching-testing nexus is one of the critical fixtures in the era of accountability in which present day educators find themselves. The full power of the state has been brought to bear on boosting test scores accompanied by broader ranges of punishments and rewards, despite the fact that teachers and administrators daily labor in the often mindless backwash that test-score improvement might mean to a healthy school life. This author has personally toured such places where a preoccupation with "the numbers" has meant mindless repetition, memorizing lists and dates over and over again, punishments, and ridicule. It is a sort of secular American madrasa mimicking what we often see on television with young, Islamic boys endlessly repeating lines from the Koran or other religious texts without thought or discussion. These are often places that breed terrorism and future suicide bombers in search of immortality in a heavenly static state. So who is responsible for this state of affairs? What responsibility does any curriculum leader have to question or resist a system of testing that is the equivalent of Franklin Bobbitt's "activity analysis"?

It is the contention of this author that curriculum leadership *does include* raising the questions about the purpose of such a system in which accountability and assessment reign supreme over almost everything else. The contemporary mantra of "data-driven decision making" is a similar chant from our secular madrasa *unless it questions the larger set of values* to which such information is connected and also asks that with the mastery of the information on the extant battery of testing tools, who really benefits from its acquisition? And since knowledge is not neutral, we also need to similarly ask, "Who doesn't benefit from its acquisition?"

To raise such questions, it is important for curriculum leaders to position curriculum content knowledge on the largest socioeconomic canvas as possible in which the schools function. It is naïve to believe that the designation of curriculum content knowledge is (a) neutral and represents the best interests of all groups of people served by the public schools equally or even equitably, and (b) all children will encounter such content knowledge in the same way based on their sociocultural group or based on the assumption that their sociocultural group is the same or if not that it makes no difference in their orientation or acquisition of it.

4.2 WHO BENEFITS FROM THE PERPETUATION OF THE CULTURAL CAPITAL EMBRACED BY STATE IMPOSED ACCOUNTABILITY MODELS?

There are different sets of values and priorities embraced by various groups in any given society. The culture that is embodied on state exams and state imposed curricula is not necessarily representative of those of all groups, and the acquisition of it as embodied on tests and in test questions privileges the groups who define them. Their definitions are a form of social control and serve to legitimize their privileged position in the larger social hierarchy. Think about it for a moment. Do you know any country where the members of the poorest or least privileged classes or groups of people define the nature of school curricula or the tests that assess it? This issue is not one of right or wrong. Human culture is a construct. It is not defined by "natural laws" but by social position. Test makers are also members of certain cultural classes. For example, in 2003, the education community was met with a charge by Jay Rosner, executive director of the Princeton Review Foundation—a group that assists poor students prepare for standardized tests—that the test questions on the SAT (Scholastic Aptitude Test) consistently favored white students. In fact, he says, "Every one of the 138 questions on the test favored white students" (Young, 2003, p. 34). Rosner says his analysis shows the same bias in previous years. He also points out that some questions not used on the SAT show that black students actually scored better than white students. Rosner denies outright racism on the part of the College Board but points out that the way the test maker defines *reliability* may be one of the causes of the achievement gap. "It's entirely internally cyclical and self-reinforcing," notes Mr. Rosner, who adds, "If they let me pick the questions, there would be a dramatic close in the gap" (Young, 2003, p. A34).

Another researcher, Roy Freedle, who worked at ETS (Educational Testing Service), which publishes the SAT, for over 30 years says that his data show that black students often did better than their white counterparts on difficult questions but did worse on the easier ones. The reason he proffered was that the easier items were, ". . . more open to interpretation based on a test taker's cultural background" (Young, 2003, p. A35), whereas the more difficult questions employed a narrower, academic vocabulary that was less open to interpretation.

The presence of cultural differences in test takers means that there is no neutral test content on some items. Some test takers will have more experience than others, a wider vocabulary, and a deeper cultural linguistic and symbolic pool upon which to draw when interpreting test questions. Bourdieu (1984) has defined cultural capital as "a form of knowledge, an internalized code or a cognitive acquisition that equips the social agent with empathy towards, appreciation for, or competence in deciphering cultural relations and cultural artifacts" (p. 2). There is certainly ample evidence that such differences not only exist among students within the schools but also in nearly all societies as well.

Bernstein's work (1990) on school and classroom codes in pedagogic discourse is revealing. Bernstein indicates that there are two sites that are involved in social reproduction, the school and the home. They are linked by the textbook. However, in some cases, the home cannot connect and function as a second (and reinforcing) site in which case, ". . . in as much as this does not occur, failure is highly likely" (p. 54). He discusses the aspects of the home that are "physical, discursive, and interactional, which enable children to manage or fail to manage class assumptions of the context and sites of reproduction, progression, and communication" (p. 54). Bernstein's work delves into ways middle class and lower class children react to things, that is, how they process information. There are distinctive differences that play out in reacting to school work and school defined problems. Very little of Bernstein's path-breaking research has been pursued in understanding the issue of the achievement gap.

4.3 AVOIDING DEFICIT MINDSETS, MODELS, AND CULTURAL MARGINALIZATION OF OTHERS

One of the major issues in discussing alignment and the achievement gap is that it is all too easy to fall into the old traps of thinking about such differences as hereditary. This is especially the case when reconceptualizing the gap in cultural capital between groups. Some of those who speak of a gap as a difference in cultural capital sometimes assume that those scoring lower are just ignorant of the ways of the world, and/or they really see them as stupid, ignorant, or lazy. While they may speak of "cultural capital," what they really mean is "genetic capacity." This is not what is meant by a discussion of cultural capital in this book. What Bourdieu's (1984) work tells us is that culture is a human construct, and those in power simply impose their view of the "proper" or "best" culture on everyone else. This is Bourdieu's concept of the *cultural arbitrary*, which contains "an implicit pedagogy capable of instilling a whole cosmology, an ethic, a metaphysic, a political philosophy" through which its imposition remains largely hidden but requires "submission to the established order" (Bourdieu, 2008, pp. 94–95).

When thinking about differences between groups and especially those who come to the school in a position of disjunction to the dominant forms of cultural capital contained in the curriculum and school routines, it is all too easy for practitioners and curriculum leaders to become arrogant, "which assigns the native person the status of an object of thought, incapable of many things: incapable of improvising new patterns of behavior . . . and incapable of possessing an even partial understanding of what is being done" (Pinto, 1999, p.101). When some children become "objects," they can be dehumanized, marginalized, and victimized. How professionals come to see what the causes of the achievement gap may be will say a lot about what happens next in trying to deal with this phenomenon.

Undoubtedly, Bourdieu's perspective will be stoutly resisted by those who see it as an attack and or rejection of cherished "Western values" and "artistic distinctions." It is simply impossible for such individuals to see the Western heritage in any other terms but sacred and divinely defined or inspired. Bourdieu and Passeron (2000) inform us that the *cultural arbitrary* is not better or worse than other cultural arbitraries, but it is different. Part of the Western heritage is also an artistic form of racism in which beauty is defined anatomically and becomes an ideal in which those that are different are held up as ugly. Cornel West (1999) has discussed how Greek models became the basis for arranging peoples of the world on a continuum of what was considered not only beautiful but human. It became "the normative gaze" by which people were measured (p. 75). Thus the thin lips and anatomical and physiognomy of the Greeks became the *cultural arbitrary* for the placement on those dimensions for the rest of humanity. If those who paint themselves and their likenesses in public places are also militarily and politically dominant, their lense becomes the way of the world and how it comes to see itself compared to those images. It would be naïve to believe that the tests in use today in our schools are not part and parcel of the same system of cultural symbols, values, and hierarchies. They are inseparable. One of the first applications of standardized exams was in China in the seventh century when job seekers for government positions had to "write essays about Confucian philosophy and compose poetry" (Mathews, 2006, p. A6). Here is one of the earliest historical examples of the use of testing in which we see the examination process anchored in a specific *cultural arbitrary,* that is, Confucian philosophy.

The important point is that we do not envision cultural differences as stable, fixed, or genetically predetermined. Rather, cultural systems are flexible and malleable, some more than others, but that they are very arbitrary. The whole system of schooling is an arbitrary process of selected and constructed experiences that represent an imposition, and as Bourdieu and Passeron (2000) have described, a form of *symbolic violence* in which a specific representation is legitimized for application in a formal system of education and serves as a mechanism for a continuing and a sanctified mechanism for social reproduction. One form of that legitimization is the school curriculum.

In nearly every society, the form and shape of cultural capital that serves the interests of those in control are attached to measures of material wealth. It is the rich people of the world who shape what schooling is for the rest of humanity. Their wealth is defined, enshrined, sanctified, legitimized, and protected by the dominant system of education in their respective societies. No system of schooling would be acceptable to them that jeopardized their hierarchical position or political power. The knowledge they approve and defend has been characterized by Foucault (1980) as *power knowledge.*

4.4 Not All Data Are Valuable or Relevant

All data do not measure the most important things, and some of it may be trivial, misleading, or unimportant. To begin with, it is clear that tests do not assess the full scope of any curriculum. It is also clear that because much curriculum is written ambiguously, when a test maker goes to develop test questions, the actual learning desired from the perspective of the curriculum developer is changed in the assessment process. Refinement can become redefinition. The disconnect between teaching, learning, and testing often occurs right at this juncture. The lack of alignment at the state level, where tests and curriculum are supposed to be congruent, has been a persistent problem (see Webb, 1997; 1999; 2002). The short cuts many state departments of education take to prepare statewide tests also eliminates the appropriate number of items that would enable them to be more accurate and fairer. And it isn't so much what the data tell you but rather understanding the reasons behind data trends. And these are not always obvious or transparent.

For example, mean differences in test scores between groups may reveal that one group is below or above another, but they don't explain why this may be so. Figure 4.1 is a representative schema of how to approach understanding the potential causes of achievement differences on test scores in a hypothetical school or school system. Figure 4.1 assumes that test information can be disaggregated by individual students, which may not always be the case. The advantages of possessing student level data are that (1) they deal with the issue of student mobility, that is, which students actually experienced any given curriculum for a specified period of time, and that (2) specific features of a curriculum can be assessed as they impact specific students. For example, if some curricula were to be taught inductively, that feature may be assessed compared to curricula not so

Figure 4.1 Determining Possible Causes of Achievement Differences on Test Scores

Data Trend	Probable Causes	Actions to Consider	Commentary
	External	External	
Test scores show that some students identified by race and/or gender show a persistent pattern of lower achievement in a specifically tested area.	(a) Were these students taught a different curriculum in some way? Were they tracked? Was the alignment to the test different, lower?	(a) Do some *curriculum mapping* to determine the actual taught curriculum. Abolish tracking. Check to ascertain actual alignment.	This is a process of elimination. Don't guess. Take every step to assure that each possible variable is included in your analysis.
	(b) Were teacher expectations different? Lower?	(b) Ensure teacher expectations were the same.	Teacher expectations for student learning can be extremely subtle and sometimes unconscious. The drop off in expectations for learning can be related to accepting any and all kinds of excuses for not performing. In some cases, teacher expectations are overt when they may say, "Those children just can't learn that."
	(c) Was the quality of teaching high? The same? Lower? Was teaching sufficiently differentiated to take into account important differences among students?	(c) Perform observations to ensure quality was similar and high. Work to ensure that teachers have at least the same expectations for all students to succeed. Followed by classroom walk-throughs with reflective conversations.	Often, instructional materials are not at the same cognitive levels as test items, meaning teaching is at one level and testing at another, even if the same content material matched.

Data Trend	Probable Causes	Actions to Consider	Commentary
	External	External	
	(d) Was the time spent on the curriculum adequate to attain at least test level mastery? Were instructional materials aligned to the curriculum and the test?	(d) By checking time spent and test results, determine if test mastery levels were met. Perform an alignment check on content, context, and cognitive level of the available instructional materials to those in the curriculum and the test.	A check for time is not a precise calculation but one that may occur in stages.
	(e) How many items on the test assessed this learning? What was the weight of the tested areas within the overall test?	(e) Determine the content weight of the test to ascertain what are the most and least frequently assessed concepts to match the emphasis in classroom instruction.	This analysis may be difficult in some states because of the paucity of information various state agencies are willing to share with local school districts regarding internal test weights.

(Continued)

Figure 4.1 (Continued)

Data Trend	Probable Causes	Actions to Consider	Commentary
	Internal	*Internal*	*Commentary*
	(f) Was the cultural capital brought by the students the same or different than all others? If different, in what way? What would be their level of familiarity of their cultural capital with the curriculum? The textbook? The test?	(f) Obvious forms of cultural capital can be recognized by wealth level of the students followed by linguistic usage.	Some forms of cultural capital are nonverbal and very subtle. Persons familiar with any given culture should be consulted.
	(g) Were cultural differences respected, or were they considered a deficit? Were they taken into account in designing classroom experiences?	(g) The teacher should try and use as many different ways as possible in designing learning to be inclusive with many cultural examples.	It should be remembered that cultures are not superior or inferior; they are simply different. Great care should be taken to avoid placing some children in deficit circumstances that amount to imposing a surrogate genetic inferiority.

designed; specific features of individual students may be related to specific curricula such as the students socioeconomic background, and it may have impacted test performance (see Solomon, Booker, & Goldhaber, 2009, for an example).

Figure 4.1 is illustrative of a rather typical scenario facing curriculum leaders in confronting the achievement gap dilemma. It breaks the problem down by those variables that are external to the learner, such as the alignment of curriculum-teaching-testing nexus and those that are internal to the learner, for example the differences in forms of cultural capital students may possess prior to encountering school defined contexts.

In this example, the test and its content have been determined by the state or some agency external to the school or the school district. Therefore, the avenue open to the teachers, administrators, and curriculum leaders is not usually one of challenging the efficacy of the test itself. So essentially the "adjustments" made by school-level or even district-level personnel represent a classic "backload" problem. In addition, the antidote in similar scenarios, such as this one, narrows the potential solutions to "tightening" the connectivity between curriculum, teaching, and testing. These are factors "external" to establishing the conditions of optimizing testing performance by ensuring that curricular ambiguity is minimized, teaching congruity to that curriculum is maximized, and that curricular-test alignment is optimized. The final factor is that learning mastery is part of this triumvirate and that time is allotted for illustrating mastery differences among students and that teaching is sufficiently differentiated so that strategies employed in the past are not repeated, in which failure occurred the first time. In this part of the solution, such factors are "loosened" and not tightened. This is the "paradox of administration," that is, knowing what variables must be tightened and which ones are to be loosened (see Thompson, 1967, p.150). Figure 4.2 is an illustration of this paradox in action.

Figure 4.2 shows the total system dynamic concerning how to envision the existence of "slack" in a school system. Slack may be considered a form or organizational variance or space. In most curricular-testing-teaching scenarios, the necessary response is to "tighten" the relationship, which results in the reduction of variance or slack in the organization. The logical institutional response to an imposed system of centralized high-stakes testing is to remove ambiguity, thus ensuring that actions, reactions, and responses are tightly coordinated and connected. The traditions in most school systems,

Figure 4.2   School System

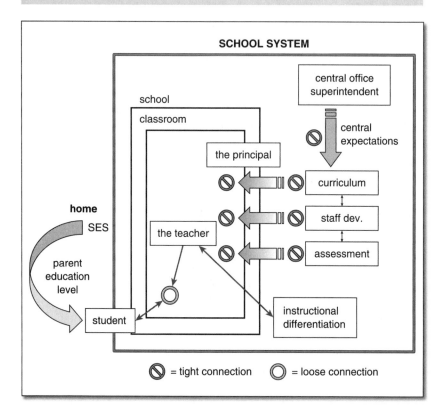

however, have been to permit much looser connections (see Weick, 1978). There will be a range of resistance to forcing closer coordination for a variety of reasons. If the school system has been one in which key functions (curriculum, personnel, finance, transportation, student services, human resource development, etc.) have come to represent "silos" with their own administrative hierarchies and budgets, reorganization will be contentions, difficult, and very political.

Taking on that part of the *achievement gap* issue, which can be attributed to organizational and/or structural problems and the existence of managerial slack in the central office, has not been well recognized until recently with curriculum audits of some large U.S. school systems (see English, 2008; English & Steffy, 2005) and sketched out in the management study conducted by Snipes, Doolittle, and Herlihy (2002) for the Council for Great City Schools.

Figure 4.2 also shows that while the response of the school system generally is to tighten connections between critical organizational functions at the classroom and/or school level, the response must be to "loosen" and to allow organizational slack to exist in which the classroom teacher is expected to engage in instructional differentiation. But there is also a paradox here. The teacher is expected to retain a tight connection to the approved curriculum (low to no slack) and to simultaneously have a rather wide range of professional latitude in determining curricular delivery. This is an extension of the design and delivery discussion in Chapter 1.

4.5 AVOIDING OUTMODED MANAGEMENT MODELS

As the reader is examining Figure 4.1 and the possible actions to pursue in closing the *achievement gap,* it is important not to simply put these actions into the traditional and existing models of management and supervision. These must also be reconceptualized. This fact is certainly not obvious because the solutions embodied in Figure 4.1 are largely rational and/or technical and can be undertaken without considering any larger ramifications or organizational changes. They should not be.

Perhaps the most striking organizational and/or managerial dilemma that confronting the *achievement gap* problem reveals from curriculum audits is that the usual way of differentiating managerial functions traditionally has been to separate line and staff in the larger administrative structure. This separation is based on classical and well-accepted managerial thinking over time (Bridges, Olm, & Barnhill, 1971, pp. 76, 85; Haire, 1964, pp. 297–299; Jackson & Morgan, 1982, pp. 140–142). But here is the dilemma as reported in large U.S. school systems in aligning the written, taught, and tested curricula from teachers and administrators who have been interviewed within the audit process.

Central office subject content specialists who write the curriculum and align it so that there is a tight connection to the tested curricula have little to no authority in the fidelity of the implementation of that curriculum. Thus, while the central office "staff" and "support" function have taken steps to ensure alignment in curriculum design, if implementation does not ensure fidelity to the design, the advantages are lost to the system. This happens when principals or their supervisors do not really understand that loose implementation (this does not mean differentiation of instruction but curriculum content variance) does not facilitate alignment but may detract from it. The purpose of alignment is to ensure that students are not surprised by tests because they have not been taught the test content or are unfamiliar with the test format (context). The most common way this happens is to permit wide variance in textbook adoption. Unfortunately, most principals see textbooks as instruction instead of curriculum. Textbooks actually are a form of curricular surrogates as long as they include curriculum content, which nearly all do. Unless a school system has determined which textbooks have the highest alignment to the required forms of assessment, alignment attained by design in the central office is eroded or erased by alignment lost to loose textbook adoption.

The organizational dilemma is that those who design a curriculum have no authority in the delivery of curriculum. This predicament has its basis in the separation of line and staff. To confront the organizational dilemma, it has been necessary to combine both of them in new configurations of administrative duties. Sometimes, this has been to rethink organization roles by re-titling a function such as "Chief Academic Officer" instead of "Associate Superintendent for Curriculum." However, sometimes this change is in name only and does not actually change anything. It all depends on what the new duties are and what authority the role has to resolve the line and/or staff dichotomy.

Another issue pertains to the traditional model of supervision that one typically finds in schools today.

4.6 UNDERSTANDING THE DRAWBACKS OF TOP-DOWN SUPERVISORY APPROACHES

Another issue with confronting the achievement gap dilemma is that the supervisory approaches typically employed in education are relics from the nineteenth century factory models in which floor foremen exercised "oversight" of workers on the shop floor and later the assembly line. The model was one in which an "errant" worker missed a required action or went to sleep or otherwise engaged in nonproductive activity and had to be immediately "corrected" in order to keep overall production going. This approach to "supervision" is embedded in a hierarchical nonreciprocal relationship in which the "supervisor" has near total power over the relationship and is expected to point out the errors of the ways of the worker.

It is this authoritarian and one-way relationship that is still used in schools today, despite the fact that the actual education levels between classroom teachers and their principals is not very large and that subject specialist teachers may know considerably more than their principals. So how is the principal going to "correct" the errors of the teacher in such circumstances?

One answer is that the lines of engagement of the principal and the teacher are not usually along curricular subject matter lines but rather general lines of instructional work. Principals typically "evaluate" teachers regarding their ability to motivate students, create interesting classroom environments, send relatively few students to the principal's office for disciplinary actions, and now with high-stakes testing, have their students score well on these instruments. In this situation, high-stakes tests become the ultimate cudgel in reinforcing the power and authority of the administration and ultimately of the existing division of labor and authority in the schools. This is especially the case when the only logical action to be taken by school-level personnel is *backloading,* that is, they have no ability to change or influence the curriculum to be tested or the instrument to be devised to assess it. Their role is simply to deliver the curriculum better.

One antidote to this problem is the Downey classroom walk-through model (Downey, Steffy, English, Frase, & Poston, 2004). The Downey model does two important things to alter the traditional top-down factory model of supervision: (1) it changes the roles of the teacher and principal from a top-down to a more equalitarian relationship via the reflective questioning practice, and (2) it requires the principal to become more knowledgeable about the actual curriculum being delivered in the classroom. Other models of classroom walk-throughs without the reflective questioning approach and which use checklists are simply technological advances in the traditional top-down model.

The advantage of the reflective approach to working relationships with teachers is that there is no "correct" or "right" answer. In this circumstance, the conversation between principals and teachers about classroom work is more about context and decisions in context than "this was good" and "this needs to be improved" one-way management mandate. A truly reflective question is centered on understanding and growing more proficient overall than in precision for the moment. It is, to harken back to a common management metaphor, more focused on "doing the right thing" as opposed to "doing it right." What is the right thing? How would one know if it were "the right thing"? A reflective question is much more apt to serve as a lever for a truly professional conversation than the more common management model commentary.

The Downey model also requires the principal to become knowledgeable about the curriculum that is to be taught. If the principal doesn't really know what math skills are to be mastered at a particular grade level or curricular location, the teacher may be highly motivational and the students engaged, but it may be for naught if students are tested on something else. We have already seen how high-stakes tests require greater alignment with classroom instruction than other kinds of assessments. Space between the content of the classroom and the content of the tests is slack and a potential source of variance to be narrowed or eliminated. On-the-other-hand, variance for method is required. This is the "tight-loose" paradox that must be understood and managed.

Much of this discussion regarding variance and its sources in schools in the teaching and testing dyad will make some individuals very nervous or negative. The decidedly "tight" fit that high-stakes testing imposes on schools is not only uncomfortable for them but restrictive. There can be no doubt about that. It is a situation not understood very well at all by many legislators and policy wonks that seem to believe that they can have high test scores and classroom freedom for everyone to be happy. Few individuals who have not worked in schools and felt the heavy hand that such testing imposes on teachers, classrooms, curricular choices, and administrative actions really understand how such impositions not only change the actual work but also often impose a truly sterile working climate and often give students the wrong idea about the purpose of schooling. It is to this agenda we now turn.

4.7 THE NEXUS OF CURRICULUM LEADERSHIP

Deciding what to teach and test is the nexus of curriculum leadership because it is at this juncture every question about the nature of education, its larger purposes and what we know about human learning and growth and development, is relevant and immediate. Teaching and testing require forthright decisions. But a thoughtful professional educator and a responsible decision maker about them requires more than rational, technical knowledge of how alignment works, how to construct user-friendly curriculum guides, or knowledge of test validity and reliability. So much more is involved at this nexus because it is simply the starting point for what is hoped for and should be some sustained, meaningful, and deep discussions about why we care about tests results in the first place. One thing should be clear. Children are not the *means* to obtain better test scores, though in some scenarios this may be true. Rather, children are the ends of what education is about in the first place. And since tests can never be a complete assessment of them or their learning (or their inherent worth, ever), test scores should be viewed with great humility, deep skepticism, and sustained temporality. There are so many stories of accomplished people who didn't test well—for example, Winston Churchill who sat through an exam for two hours and only put his name on the paper before his blank sheets were collected and was thereafter "consigned to a sort of remedial class for dullards" (Keegan, 2002, pp. 25–26). Another "plodding, lackluster student, with no discernible trace of brilliance" according to his biographer, was the financial titan John D. Rockefeller Senior (Chernow, 1998, p. 34). Still another world historic figure had troubles with his multiplication tables and in recollection of his school days recalled he was a mediocre student. He ran home from school each day so as not to have to talk to anyone because, "I was even afraid lest anyone should poke fun at me" (Fischer, 1950, p. 16). He took up smoking and stole money to buy cigarettes. Once, he made a spelling mistake and was scolded by his teacher because he held the class back from a perfect record. He was later to be called "the Mahatma" and led his country to freedom within the British Empire.

There are more paradoxes as well. As I have sketched out in this book, *curriculum alignment* is a sound educational choice when up against the conditions imposed by governmental agencies regarding test score targets. There are few other options available. Yet even without such targets and mandates, alignment is a logical choice. Why would a teacher teach one thing and test students on something else? Why would teachers teach one way and test student some other way? Alignment is not only good practice but also *fair practice*. Alignment makes sense outside of the political practices and strictures of the current times because it is at the heart of a trusting relationship between teachers and students. In essence, it means, from the student's perspective, "I trust that you will teach me what you will test me on and that you will not trick me or embarrass me in the process."

4.8 Some Concluding Thoughts

The first edition of *Deciding What to Teach and Test* was written nearly 20 years ago. Since that time, the trends that prompted its publication have continued unabated and even intensified. Yet even with the practices described in this revised edition, there are differences between students within various subcultures, intermingled with linguistic practices, that will continue to be reflected in test scores based on assumptions of monoculturalism. There are tantalizing clues that should be investigated by government research agencies and foundations. For example, the U.S. school system is regularly ranked in comparative educational test scores behind a dozen other nations and is roundly condemned as a failure (Levin & Holmes, 2005; Tomsho, 2009). Yet what ought to be remembered is that the United States does not have a truly national system of education. We have no common curriculum for the 50 states and no common test of that curriculum. The states regularly change the standards and the testing score indicators (see Hechinger, 2009b). When some of the states break out their test scores apart from the United States as a whole, a different picture emerges. For example, Massachusetts and Minnesota compared their scores separately and were ahead of the United States as a whole. In fact, "Massachusetts fourth graders scored roughly as well as those in high-performing Taiwan and Japan—the third- and fourth-ranked nations of the world in math in 2007 (Hechinger, 2008, D1). So not all states and local school systems are doing poorly. It is only in the inner cities and some rural areas that lower scores emerge. American education as a whole is falsely condemned when it does not even qualify as a national system of education. Questions need to be generated from this knowledge, however. The research of Bourdieu and Passeron (2000) and that of Bernstein (1990, 1996) should be employed to pursue why cultural and racial diversity crop up in such comparisons and why nations with much lower diversity such as Hong Kong, Singapore, Taiwan, and Japan are the top math scorers in the world. But the fact is that some parts of U.S. education are doing just fine by international test score comparisons, thank you.

However, among the more practical matters are how do test questions assume cultural homogeneity among test takers? How do the lived cultural experiences of various children in different cultures account for test-score variance and in what ways? How do school codes and pedagogical practices place some students at an advantage and others at a disadvantage? How do power relations within the larger social structure and within the schools legitimate inequalities and place some classes of students consistently reaping a greater slice of the educational rewards than others?

How do statistical procedures that show good reliability work against cultural differences in respondents? Are statistical procedures dependent and/or improved as measures with assumptions of monoculturalism? If test scores show high correlations to material wealth, how can wealth and its attendant cultural acquisitions and linguistic variances be fair measures of school success with low wealth students? How can such factors ever be truly eliminated (or "controlled" in statistical parlance) when they are embedded in *both* the test takers' backgrounds, the nature and assumptions of the tests, and the curriculum that is selected for use in the schools?

We cannot allow the testing industry to answer these questions alone. They have a huge vested interest in maintaining the facade of impartiality and meritocracy in which the profits of their industry are vouchsafed. These are issues and questions for university research, government studies, and sustained and enlightened foundation funding. However, with the exception of some university-based researchers, legislation and government programs, as well as nearly all foundation funding, perpetuate the problem instead of deconstructing their own rhetoric and interests in the same old models and solutions. This is a colossal failure and a potential tragedy of immense proportions for our schools.

The last place we can hope to find some resilience in standing up to these formidable forces is represented by local educational practitioners, the people for whom this book has been written, the people who stand at the nexus of the deciding what to teach and test junction in our schools. If another 20 years should pass, let us hope that the emergence of some new thinking, new discoveries, and real progress on the achievement gap will have occurred. In short, it will take more than courage. It will take unlocking some long histories and entrenched interests for which all of the parties who have a vested position in the status quo will strenuously resist and work to discredit. However, some of the children of America deserve a better education than many are now receiving. But to provide it, we will have to look very hard at the larger socioeconomic structure that positions many of them in a subservient position; for as Bernstein (1996) has cautioned us, "There is likely to be an unequal distribution of images, knowledges, possibilities, and resources that will affect the rights of participation, inclusion, and individual enhancement of groups of students. It is highly likely that the students who do not receive these rights in school come from social groups who do not receive these rights in society" (p. 8).

Glossary of Terms

Articulation of curriculum. When a curriculum is "articulated," it is focused and connected vertically from one grade to the next or from one school to the next. Another synonym for articulation is *continuity. Consistency* is a synonym for *coordination.*

Backloading. This means that one engages in alignment by beginning with the test and working "back" to the curriculum. In this case, the test developers are also the persons who write the curriculum. The major advantage to backloading is that it is quick and relatively inexpensive compared with the "frontloading" process. The reason is that an entire curriculum does not have to be written before alignment can take place.

Content and context alignment. Alignment between the test and the curriculum occurs at two levels. The first is called *content alignment* and refers to the situation where the test content and the curriculum content are the same. The second, *context alignment* (sometimes called *format alignment*), means that the testing protocol or scenario is the same as the one in the curriculum or work plan (textbook). A third level of alignment is *level of cognition* that refers to the match of cognitive levels between the written curriculum, taught curriculum, and tested curriculum.

Coordination of curriculum. The lateral or horizontal focus and connectivity of curriculum in a school environment. For example, a view of all ninth-grade algebra classes might reveal a common focus and connectivity present (though not necessarily identical). In this case, the curriculum is said to be "coordinated."

Cultural arbitrary. The language, concepts, dispositions, and world views of the political elites who control the process of schooling and impose those views on the remainder of the socio-economic system. Culture is a human construct and is not "natural." Those in control of the process of education see their own culture as "natural" and seek to impose it on all others via schooling.

Cultural capital. A form of non-economic capital that represents the knowledge, depositions, manners, ways of dress, values, and deportment of self of the political elites. As such, they normally reinforce the hierarchical position of the elites in the overall socioeconomic structure.

Cultural literacy. The idea that one set of cultural knowledges, facts, and/or historical events constitutes the definition of what it means to be "educated." Such a definition is an example of Bourdieu's notion of the "cultural arbitrary" and is defined and imposed by the political elites to ensure their position in the larger sociopolitical structure.

Curriculum. The sanctioned plan of studies approved by the state or the delegated representatives of the state that divides the activities of teachers into a variety of forms for presentation and examination of the students. It consists of a formal aspect, that is, that which appears in curriculum plans, guides, and adopted textbooks and other materials; informal aspects that are the ways of thinking, speaking, and presentation of self within a given dominant culture; and a hidden aspect, which is how the culture of the political elites is legitimated and perpetuated within the schools.

Curriculum alignment. The "match" or fit between the curriculum (in whatever form it may exist) and the test or tests to be used to assess learners. This is called *design alignment* because it is usually built into the curriculum as it is being developed.

Curriculum audit. A process where an external review of the content of the curriculum is examined compared to local, state, and federal requirements; where alignment at different levels is ascertained; where assessment trends are graphed and connected to specific achievement trend lines linked to gender, race, and SES levels; and where the administrative structure is assessed as to its capacity to effectively deliver the curriculum.

Curriculum content. The body of knowledge, concepts, processes, and dispositions that are embodied in any given curriculum document. Some curriculum content can include *methodology,* that is *delivery*, if that is an integral part of the content, for example in a Socratically designed curriculum.

Curriculum evaluation. Evaluation of a curriculum may consist of assessing whether or not children have learned that which the curriculum indicated should be taught, or it may be an assessment of the teacher in the act of delivering the curriculum. The latter is sometimes called teacher evaluation.

Curriculum mapping. As originally used in the 1980s, a curriculum map is a record of the actual taught curriculum and not the desired curriculum. It is a term to denote the "real" as opposed to "ought to be" curriculum.

Curriculum validation. A consensus activity in which certain curricular knowledge is voted on or matched to groups or expert individuals opinions as to which knowledge or curriculum is of most worth.

Data disaggregation. The act of taking test items and breaking them into smaller components, skills, knowledge, and content for teaching in smaller pieces and from which to adjust the curriculum or the work plan so that teaching changes as a result. Such changes may include or exclude different content, may spend more time on certain areas to teach, and may alter the scope and/or sequence of curricular content.

Data-driven decision making. The perspective that important decisions should be rooted in information related to organizational performance. The concept works only if the data are relative to performance and performance is impacted by the subsequent decisions made with it.

Design and delivery of curriculum. The *design* of the curriculum refers to the act of creating it via specification or template. A *template* is simply the criteria or requirements a curriculum must fulfill or include. These might include state law, state testing, national goals, local priorities, and a specific learning theory or grouping practice.

Frontloading. This refers to the concept of design alignment in which the curriculum and the test(s) are "matched." One would begin the matching process by first writing the curriculum and then selecting, adapting, or developing the test that "fits" the curriculum (or is aligned with it). To engage in "frontloading," an entire curriculum must be developed before alignment to any test can occur. This means that "frontloading" is the most time-consuming and expensive way to establish alignment.

Habitus. A concept from Bourdieu (1977) stating that humans grow up within certain social fields that inculcate their members with dispositions and outlooks that are distinctive to others. As humans mature within their habituses, they acquire the attitudes and values that perpetuate themselves. Humans come to believe that their habitus is "natural" and is not usually questioned. Swartz (1997) indicates that habitus "does not stand in opposition to society; it is one of its forms of existence" (p. 96).

Hidden curriculum. Refers to those values in which the selection of the curriculum content are embedded, often without question. Such values have determined what is actually selected as curriculum content. According to Bourdieu (2008), the process of selection is often *misrecognized,* even from the eyes of those proposing the content who fail to be sufficiently critical of their own stake in pursuing the goals within their power and control.

Ideology. A closed system of beliefs or values in which the original assumptions of those beliefs or values are never questioned but accepted as "givens." Most curriculum is centered on specified and accepted cultural ideologies enshrined in state curricular frameworks or guidelines and approved by official state agencies for implementation in the schools.

Knowledge. The "stuff" within a curriculum of which it is comprised. These may be facts, figures, concepts, processes, dispositions that are both overt and covert, and ways of seeing and thinking. For example, the Western practice of binary logic is usually part and parcel of the knowledge content of most curricula in the schools. An implicit assumption of curriculum knowledge is that it is a "truthful" way of seeing what "is out there" in the real world, and "this is the way it really works or the way it really happened." Rarely do such presentations question this implicit assumption, and rarely do curriculum writers believe that what they are placing within a curriculum is not "neutral" when in fact the posture of neutrality is a charade. Curriculum knowledge benefits some persons and groups and not others. It is rarely neutral in this regard. The inclusion of forms of curriculum knowledge represents a political act of choice within systems of values and interests. Most often, the selection of the content is biased toward those who are in policy control of the educational system and therefore solidifies their hierarchical hold in the larger sociopolitical realm as well.

Instruction. When teaching is influenced by or "guided by" a work plan (or curriculum), it becomes *instruction*. Instruction is focused and connected teaching. It is systematized teaching that adheres to the curriculum, and all formal testing scenarios (and tests) are implicitly based upon this teaching.

Needs assessment. A rational and/or technical process of examining pupil attainment form patterns of data and determining critical "gaps" to desired performance. These "gaps" are needs, and curriculum is specifically constructed to close the gaps or "meet the needs."

Pacing guide. A document developed at the district level that identifies specific objective or designated curriculum contents that teachers are supposed to focus on during a specified time period. There are strengths and weaknesses with the use of pacing guides.

Paradox of administration. A phenomenon in management where in order to be responsive to increased external pressures for less variance in a product or service, some relationships in the actual construction or delivery must be loosened as everything else is tightened. Flexibility and adaptation in that construction or delivery of a service requires independence of judgment and must be present for improvements to be made.

Pareto analysis. An analytical procedure in which, when examining results, one searches for patterns that undergird the largest number of errors and works to correct them instead of trying to correct all errors. Named after Vilfredo Pareto (see Powers, 1987).

Power. The legitimization and authorization within law and social institutions to define the shape of education (schooling) and to compel its use and impose its form on the remainder of those living in any given social system.

Quality control. The organizational capability through human decision making and action to tighten or loosen the connections between the *written*, *taught*, and *tested curricula* in schools and school systems and knowing when and how to accomplish it.

The rational system. The idea here is that school systems are goal driven, and the resources required to run them should be configured in such a way as to enable them to accomplish the desired or designated objectives. Organizations whose operations are directed by the desire to attain goals are called *rational* (Silver, 1983, p. 77). Curriculum management assumes that school systems are rational in nature.

Reconnecting data to the curriculum or "the reconnect." Once test or assessment data have been disaggregated, they must be "reconnected" to the work plan so that teachers have a different set of directions from which to teach. The reconnect means that test information is attached back into the curriculum, and the curriculum is altered accordingly.

Schooling. The state imposed and sanctioned system of education that is made compulsory for all students within the legally defined authority of the government. The system of schools is designed to legitimate the cultural capital of the elites who control them and the schools are an important part of legitimizing it. Schooling bestows lawfulness and authenticity to the construction and the use of social power of those in control acting in their own self-interests.

Slack. The idea that there is space or variance between organizational functions and/or services that inhibits the necessary connections to more specifically focus the work of the organization, from planning to execution.

Social capital. Social capital is the aggregate of the real or future resources that are linked to membership within a given social group in the larger network and the influence and power *of that group.*

Teacher autonomy. The political and technical space in the school or school system in which teachers are expected to exercise independent judgment about adapting instruction to deliver the state mandated curriculum, and at times, to bring that curriculum into question. This is part of the "paradox of administration," a loose-tight relationship between curriculum design and delivery.

Teacher isolation. The extent to which a teacher is not part of the necessary instructional connection in order for students to receive a consistent and continuous level of experiencing the required and tested curricula in a state approved and mandated program of studies and assessment.

"Tightening" the curriculum. Actions that bring the written, taught, and tested curricula into alignment or congruence with one another. *Tightening* means that the lack of overlap between the three curricula is decreased.

Tyler rationale. An approach advocated by Ralph Tyler (1949), a professor at the University of Chicago who created a model for curriculum development that is still in use today. The Tyler rationale includes the delineation of objectives from various knowledge bases and opining the needs of society. The approach has been subjected to sustained criticism on the grounds that it is culturally naïve and cloaked in a kind of false scientific objectivity.

References

Adler, M. J. (1982). *The Paideia proposal*. New York: Macmillan.

Allen, M. J., & Yen, W. M. (1979). *Introduction to measurement theory*. Monterey, CA: Brooks/Cole.

Anderson, G., & Pini, M. (2005). Educational leadership and the new economy: Keeping the "public" in public schools. In F. English (Ed.), *The SAGE Handbook of Educational Leadership* (pp. 216–236). Thousand Oaks, CA: SAGE.

Andrews, E. (1854). *Copious and critical Latin-English Lexicon*. New York: Harper & Brothers, Publishers.

Apple, M. W. (1979). *Ideology and curriculum*. London: Routledge & Kegan Paul.

Apple, M. W. (1986). *Teachers & texts*. New York: Routledge & Kegan Paul.

Apple, M. W. (1988). *Teachers and texts: A political economy of class and gender relations in Education*. New York: Routledge & Kegan Paul.

Arendt, H. (2006). *Eichmann in Jerusalem: A report on the banality of evil*. New York: Penguin Books.

Armstrong, R., Cornell, T. D., Kraner, R. E., & Roberson, E. W. (1970). *The development and evaluation of behavioral objectives*. Worthington, OH: C. A. Jones.

Aronowitz, S., & Giroux, H. A. (1985). *Education under siege*. South Hadley, MA: Bergin & Garvey.

Bates, S. (1993). *Battleground: One mother's crusade, the religious right, and the struggle for control of our classrooms*. New York: Poseidon Press.

Beauchamp, G. A. (1975). *Curriculum theory*. Wilmette, IL: Kagg.

Bell, T. (1988). *The thirteenth man: A Reagan cabinet memoir*. New York: The Free Press.

Bennett, W. J. (1988). *American education: Making it work*. Washington, DC: Government Printing Office.

Bernstein, B. (1990). *The structuring of pedagogic discourse: Class, codes, and control*. London: Routledge, Chapman & Hall.

Bernstein, B. (1996). *Pedagogy, symbolic control and identity: Theory, research, critique.* London, UK: Taylor & Francis.

Bernstein, H. (1985, March). The new politics of textbook adoption. *Phi Delta Kappan, 66*(7), 463–465.

Bertrand, A., & Cebula, J. P. (1980). *Tests, measurement, and evaluation.* Reading, MA: Addison-Wesley.

Bidwell, C. (1965). The school as a formal organization. In J. G. March (Ed.), *Handbook of organizations* (pp. 972–1022). Chicago: Rand McNally & Company.

Bobbitt, F. (1918, 1971). *The curriculum.* New York: Arno Press.

Bode, B. (1930). *Modern educational theories.* New York: The Macmillan Company.

Bourdieu, P. (1977). *Outline of a theory of practice.* Cambridge, UK: Cambridge University Press.

Bourdieu, P. (1984). *Distinction: A social critique of the judgment of taste.* R. Nice, *Trans.* Cambridge, MA: Harvard University Press.

Bourdieu, P. (1993). *The field of cultural production.* R. Johnson (Ed.), New York: Columbia University Press.

Bourdieu, P. (1998). *Acts of resistance: Against the tyranny of the market.* New York: The New Press.

Bourdieu, P. (2008). *Outline of a theory of practice.* Cambridge, UK: Cambridge University Press.

Bourdieu, P., & Passeron, J.-C., (2000). *Reproduction in education, society and culture* (2nd edition). London: SAGE.

Bowles, S., & Gintis, H. (1976). *Schooling in capitalist America: Educational reform and the contradictions of economic life.* New York: Basic Books.

Bridges, F., Olm, K., & Barnhill, J. (1971). *Management decisions and organizational policy.* Boston: Allyn and Bacon.

Broad Foundation & Thomas B. Fordham Institute. (2003). *Better leaders for America's schools: A manifesto.* Retrieved February 11, 2004, from http://www.edexcellence.net/doc/Manifesto.pdf

Brock, D. (2004). *The republican noise machine: Right-wing media and how it corrupts democracy.* New York: Three Rivers Press.

Burr, I. W. (1976). *Statistical quality control methods.* New York: Marcel Dekker.

Bustillo, M. (2008, December 24). Wal-Mart to settle 63 suits over wages. *The Wall Street Journal,* B1.

Cangelosi, J. S. (1991). *Evaluating classroom instruction.* New York: Longman.

Cetron, M., & Gayle, M. (1991). *Educational renaissance.* New York: St. Martin's.

Chernow, R. (1998). *Titan: The life of John D. Rockefeller, Sr.* New York: Vintage Books.

Cole, M. (Ed.) (1988). *Bowles and Gintis revisited: Correspondence and contradiction in educational theory.* London: The Falmer Press.

Coleman, J. S. (1966). *Equality of educational opportunity.* Washington, DC: Government Printing Office.

Concise Columbia Encyclopedia, 3rd ed. (1994). Chaucer, Geoffrey, 164. New York: Columbia University Press.

Conason, J. (2003). *Big lies: The right-wing propaganda machine and how it distorts the truth.* New York: Thomas Dunne Books.

Courts, P. L. (1991). *Literacy and empowerment.* South Hadley, MA: Bergin & Garvey.

Cronbach, L. J. (1963). Evaluation of course improvement. *Teachers College Record, 64,* 672–683.

Cuban, L. (2004). *The blackboard and the bottom line: Why schools can't be businesses.* Cambridge, MA: Harvard University Press.

Cumings, B. (2009, September). The North Korea problem: Dealing with irrationality. *Current History, 108*(719), 284–290.

Delfattore, J. (1992). *What Johnny shouldn't read: Textbook censorship in America.* New Haven, Ct: Yale University Press.

Downey, C., Steffy, B., English, F., Frase, L., & Poston, W. (2004). *The three-minute classroom walk-through: Changing school supervisory practice one teacher at a time.* Thousand Oaks, CA: Corwin.

Downey, C., Steffy, B., Poston, W., & English, F. (2009). *Fifty ways to close the achievement gap.* Thousand Oaks, CA: Corwin.

Dreeben, R. (1973). The school as a workplace. In R. M. W. Travers (Ed.), *Second handbook of research on teaching* (pp. 450–473). Chicago: Rand McNally.

Durkheim, E. (1956). *Education and sociology.* New York: The Free Press.

Economist, The. (2006, February 11). Wasting brains: Germany's school system fails to make the most of the country's human capital, *378*(8464), 6–7.

Eisinger, P., & Hula, R. (2008). Gunslinger school administrators: Nontraditional leadership in urban school systems in the United States. In J. Munro (Ed.), *Educational Leadership* (pp. 345–365). Boston: McGraw-Hill.

Ellis, A. K., Mackey, J. A., & Glenn, A. D. (1988). *The school curriculum.* Boston: Allyn & Bacon.

Emery, K., & Ohanian, S. (2004). *Why is corporate America bashing our public schools?* Portsmouth, NH: Heinemann.

English, F. W. (1978). *Quality control in curriculum development.* Arlington, VA: American Association of School Administrators.

English, F. W. (1980). Curriculum mapping. *Educational Leadership, 35*(79), 558–559.

English, F. W. (1987). *Curriculum management for schools, colleges, business.* Springfield, IL: Charles C. Thomas.

English, F. W. (2002, May). On the intractability of the achievement gap in urban schools and the discursive practice of continuing racial discrimination. *Education and Urban Society, 34*(3), 298–311.

English, F. W. (2008, March–April). The curriculum management audit: Making sense of organizational dynamics and paradoxes in closing the achievement gap. *Edge, 3*(4), 18.

English, F. W., & Hill, J. C. (1990). *Restructuring: The principal and curriculum change.* Reston, VA: National Association of Secondary School Principals.

English, F. W., & Larson, R. (1996). *Curriculum management for educational and social service organizations.* Springfield, IL: Charles C. Thomas Publishing.

English, F., & Steffy, B. (1983, Fall). Curriculum mapping: An aid to school curriculum management. *Spectrum, 1*(3), 17–26.

English, F. W., & Steffy, B. (2005). Curriculum leadership: The administrative survival skill in a test-driven culture and a competitive educational marketplace. In F. English (Ed.), *The SAGE handbook of educational leadership* (pp. 407–429). Thousand Oaks, CA: SAGE.

Fine, B. (1975). *The stranglehold of the IQ.* Garden City, NY: Double-Day.

Fischer, L. (1950). *The life of Mahatma Gandhi.* New York: Harper and Brothers Publishers.

Fitzgerald, F. (1979). *America revised.* Boston: Little, Brown.

Foucault, M. (1980). *Power/knowledge.* New York: Pantheon Books.

Fowler, W. J., Jr., & Walberg, H. J. (1991). School size, characteristics, and outcomes. *Educational Evaluation and Policy Analysis, 13*(2), 189–202.

Fox, L. (2003). *Enron: The rise and fall.* New York: John Wiley & Sons.

Freire, P. (2005). *Teachers as cultural workers.* Boulder, CO: Westview Press.

Gagne, R. M., & Briggs, L. J. (1979). *Principles of instructional design.* New York: Holt, Rinehart & Winston.

Gerstner, L. (2008, December 1). Lessons from 40 years of educational "reform." *The Wall Street Journal,* A23.

Gerth, H., & Mills, C. (1970). *From Max Weber: Essays in sociology.* New York: Oxford University Press.

Giroux, H. (1988). *Teachers as intellectuals.* New York: Bergin & Garvey.

Glatthorn, A. (1987). *Curriculum leadership.* Glenview, IL: Scott, Foresman.

Goldstein, P. (1978). *Changing the American schoolbook.* Lexington, MA: D. C. Heath.

Groopman, J. (2010, February 11). Health care: Who knows "best"? *The New York Review of Books, 57*(2), 12-15.

Guilford, J. P. (1936). *Psychometric methods.* New York: McGraw-Hill.

Haire, M. (1964). *Modern organization theory.* New York: John Wiley & Sons.

Haladyna, T. M., Nolen, S. B., & Haas, N. S. (1991). Raising standardized achievement test scores and the origins of test score pollution. *Educational Researcher, 20*(5), 2–7.

Hall, E. (1977). *Beyond culture.* Garden City, NY: Anchor.

Hechinger, J. (2008, December 10). U.S. students make gains in math scores. *The Wall Street Journal,* D1, D2.

Hechinger, J. (2009a, May 20). SAT coaching found to boost scores-barely. *The Wall Street Journal,* p. D1, D7.

Hechinger, J. (2009b, October 30). Some states drop testing bar. *The Wall Street Journal,* A3.

House, E., & Haug, R. (1995). Riding "The bell curve:" A review. *Educational Evaluation and Policy Analysis, 17*(2), 263–272.

Hernstein, R., & Murray, C. (2004). *The bell curve.* New York: Free Press.

Hess, F. (2004). A license to lead? In T. Lasley (Ed.), *Better leaders for America's schools: Perspectives on the Manifesto* (UCEA Monograph, pp. 36–51) Columbia, MO: UCEA.

Hirsch, E. (1988). *Cultural literacy.* New York: Vintage Books.

Horton, G. (2003, April 25). An insider's view of "A nation at risk" and why it still matters. *The Chronicle of Higher Education, 49*(33), B13–B15.

Hunkins, F. P. (1980). *Curriculum development.* Columbus, OH: Charles E. Merrill.

Ingersoll, R. (2003). *Who controls teachers' work?* Cambridge, MA: Harvard University Press.

Jackson, J., & Morgan, C. (1982). *Organization theory: A macro perspective for management.* Englewood Cliffs, NJ: Prentice-Hall.

Jacobs, H. (1997). *Mapping the big picture: Integrating curriculum and assessment K–12.* Alexandria, VA: Association of Supervision and Curriculum Development.

Jencks, C. (1972). *Inequality.* New York: Basic Books.

Jencks, C., & Phillips, M. (1998). *The black-white test score gap.* Washington, DC: Brookings Institution Press.

Jensen, A. R. (1980). *Bias in mental testing.* New York: Free Press.

Johnson, R. (Ed.) *The field of cultural production: Essays on art and literature: Pierre Bourdieu.* New York: Columbia University Press.

Katz, M. B. (1987). *Reconstructing American education.* Cambridge, MA: Harvard University Press.

Kaufman, R., & English, F. W. (1979). *Needs assessment: Concept and application.* Englewood Cliffs, NJ: Educational Technology.

Kaufman, R., & Herman, J. (1991). *Strategic planning in education.* Lancaster, PA: Technomic.

Keegan, J. (2002). *Winston Churchill.* New York: AA Lipper Viking Book.

Kerbo, H. (1983). Social stratification and inequality: Class conflict in the United States.

Keith, S. (1991). The determinants of textbook content. In P. Altbach, G. Kelly, H. Petrie, & L. Weis (Eds.), *Textbooks in American society* (pp. 43–59). Albany, NY: SUNY Press.

Kevles, D. (1999). *In the name of eugenics: Genetics and the uses of human heredity.* Cambridge, MA: Harvard University Press.

Khurana, R. (2007). *From higher aims to hired hands: The social transformation of American business schools and the unfilled promise of management as a profession.* Princeton, NJ: Princeton University Press.

Kincheloe, J., & Steinberg, S. (1997). Who said it can't happen here? In J. Kincheloe, S. Steinberg, & A. Gresson (Eds.), *Measured lies: The bell curve examined* (pp. 3–50). New York: St. Martin's Press.

Klausmeier, H. J., & Goodwin, W. (1966). *Learning and human abilities.* New York: Harper & Row.

Kliebard, H. (1985). Three concerns of American curriculum thought. In A. Molnar (Ed.), *Current thought on curriculum* (pp. 31–44). Alexandria, VA: Association of Supervision and Curriculum Development.

Klineberg, O. (1935). *Race differences.* New York: Harper.

Kronholz, J. (2002, July 18). No pimples, pools, or pop. *The Wall Street Journal,* B1.

Lauricella, T. (2004, January 8). Scandal reaches far and high. *The Wall Street Journal,* R1, R4.

Levin, H., & Holmes, N. (2005, November 7). America's learning deficit. *New York Times,* A25.

Levitt, A., & Breeden, R. (2003, December 3). Our ethical erosion. *The Wall Street,* A16.

Lien, A. J. (1976). *Measurement and evaluation of learning.* Dubuque, IA: William C. Brown.

Lincoln, E. A. (1924). *Beginnings in educational measurement.* Philadelphia: J. B. Lippincott.

Lincoln, Y. (1997). For whom *The Bell* tolls: A cognitive or educated elite? In J. Kincheloe, S. Steinberg, & A. Gresson (Eds.), *Measured lies: The Bell Curve examined* (pp.127–136). New York: St. Martin's Press.

Lincoln, Y. S., & Guba, E. G. (1985). *Naturalistic inquiry.* Beverly Hills, CA: SAGE.

Lind, J. (2009, May/June). The perils of apology. *Foreign Affairs, 88*(3), 132–146.

Lortie, D. (1975). *Schoolteacher: A sociological study.* Chicago: The University of Chicago Press.

Lyman, H. B. (1971). *Test scores and what they mean.* Englewood Cliffs, NJ: Prentice-Hall.

Madaus, G., & Kellaghan, T. (1992). Curriculum evaluation and assessment. In P. Jackson (Ed.), *Handbook of research on curriculum* (pp. 119–156). New York: Maxwell Macmillan International.

Mager, R. (1962). *Preparing objectives for programmed instruction.* San Francisco: Fearon.

Magnusson, D. (1966). *Test theory.* Reading, MA: Addison-Wesley.

Marks, R. (1981). *The idea of IQ.* Washington, DC: University Press of America.

Mathews, J. (2006, November 14). Just whose idea was all this testing? *The Washington Post,* A6.

Maxcy, S. J. (1991). *Educational leadership.* South Hadley, MA: Bergin & Garvey.

McLaren, P. (1986). *Schooling as a ritual performance.* London: Routledge & Kegan Paul.

McNeil, J. D. (1977). *Curriculum.* Boston: Little, Brown.

McNeil, L. (2000). *Contradictions of school reform: Educational costs of standardized testing.* New York: Routledge.

Medeiros, E. (2009, September). Is Beijing ready for global leadership? *Current History, 108*(719), 250–256.

Mehrens, W. A., & Kaminski, J. (1988). *Using commercial test preparation materials for improving standardized test scores: Fruitful, fruitless, or fraudulent?* East Lansing: Michigan State University School of Education.

Mehrens, W. A., & Lehmann, I. J. (1987). *Using standardized tests in education.* New York: Longman.

Mirande, A., & Enriquez, E. (1979). *La Chicana.* Chicago: University of Chicago Press.

Mitchell, C., & Weiler, K. (1991). *Rewriting literacy.* South Hadley, MA: Bergin & Garvey.

Mohawk, J. (2000). *Utopian legacies: A history of conquest and oppression in the western world.* Santa Fe, New Mexico: Clear Light Publishers.

Montejano, D. (1987). *Anglos and Mexicans.* Austin: University of Texas Press.

Morrison, P. (1977). The bell shaped pitfall. In P. L. Houts (Ed.), *The myth of measurability.* New York: Hart.

Moss-Mitchell, F. (1998). *The effects of curriculum alignment on the mathematics achievement of third-grade students as measured by the Iowa Tests of Basic Skills: Implications for educational administrators.* Unpublished doctoral dissertation, Clark Atlanta University.

Nash, G., Crabtree, C., & Dunn, R. (1997). *History on trial: Culture wars and the teaching of the past.* New York: Alfred A. Knopf.

National Commission on Excellence in Education. (1983). *A nation at risk: The imperative of educational reform.* Washington, DC U.S. Department of Education.

Niedermeyer, F., & Yelon, S. (1981). Los Angeles aligns instruction with essential skills. *Educational Leadership, 38*(8), 618–620.

Nietz, J. (1966). *The evolution of American secondary school textbooks.* Rutland, VT: Charles E. Tuttle Company.

O'Neill, W. F. (1981). *Educational ideologies.* Santa Monica, CA: Goodyear.

Parenti, M. (1978). *Power and the powerless.* New York: St. Martin's Press.

Parkay, F., Hass, G., & Anctil, E. (2010). *Curriculum leadership.* Boston: Allyn & Bacon.

Payne, D. A. (1968). *The specification and measurement of learning outcomes.* Waltham, MA: Blaisdell.

Perkinson, H. (1985). American textbooks and educational change. In D. Svobodny (Ed.) *Early American textbooks, 1775–1900.* Washington, D.C. U.S. Department of Education.

Peters, T. J., & Waterman, R. H. (1982). *In search of excellence.* New York: Harper & Row.

Pinto, L. (1999). Theory in practice. In R. Chusterman (Ed.), *Bourdieu: A critical reader.* (pp. 95–112) Cambride, UK: Blackwell Publishers.

Popham, J. (1981). *Modern educational measurement.* Englewood Cliffs, NJ: Prentice-Hall.

Pounds, R. L. (1968). *The development of education in Western culture.* New York: Appleton-Century-Crofts.

Powers, C. H. (1987). *Vilfredo Pareto.* Newbury Park, CA: SAGE.

Price-Baugh, R. (1997). *Correlation of textbook alignment with student achievement scores.* Unpublished doctoral dissertation. Baylor University.

Purpel, D. E. (1988). *The moral and spiritual crisis in education.* South Hadley, MA: Bergin & Garvey.

Ravitch, D. (1974). *The great school wars: New York City, 1805–1973.* New York: Basic Books.

Ravitch, D. (2004). *The language police: How pressure groups restrict what students learn.* New York: Vintage Books.

Resnick, D. P., & Resnick, L. B. (1985). Standards, curriculum, and performance: A historical and comparative perspective. *Educational Researcher; 14*(4), 5–21.

Riley, N. (2009, August 29). "We're in the venture philanthropy business." *The Wall Street Journal,* A11.

Rugg, H. (1941). *That men may understand: An American in the long armistice.* New York: Doubleday, Doran.

Rutter, M., Maughan, B., Mortimore, P., Ouston, J., & Smith, A. (1979). *Fifteen thousand hours: Secondary schools and their effects on children.* Cambridge, MA: Harvard University Press.

Sacks, P. (1997, March/April). Standardized testing: Meritocracy's crooked yardstick. *Change,* pp. 25–28.

Samuda, R. J. (1975). *Psychological testing of American minorities.* New York: Dodd, Mead.

Sarason, S. (1990). *The predictable failure of educational reform.* San Francisco: Jossey-Bass.

Sax, G. (1980). *Principles of educational and psychological measurement and evaluation.* Belmont, CA: Wadsworth.

Schubert, W. (1980). *Curriculum books: The first eighty years.* Washington, D.C. University Press of America.

Schubert, W. H. (1986). *Curriculum.* New York: Macmillan.

Swartz, D. (1997). *Culture and power: The sociology of Pierre Bourdieu.* Chicago: University of Chicago Press.

Shannon, P. (1988). *Broken promises: Reading instruction in twentieth-century America.* South Hadley, MA: Bergin & Garvey.

Shor, I. (1986). *Culture wars: School and society in the conservative restoration 1969–1984.* Boston, MA: Routledge & Kegan Paul.

Silver, P. (1983). *Educational administration.* New York: Harper and Row.

Simon, R. I., Dippo, D., & Schenke, A. (1991). *Learning work.* South Hadley, MA: Bergin & Garvey.

Simon, W. (2009, December 21). Andean nations seek revival for ancient Inca tongue. *Buenos Aires Herald, 134*(12025), 15.

Smith, M. L. (1991). Meanings of test preparation. *American Educational Research Journal, 28*(3), 521–542.

Smith, M., & Rottenberg, C. (1991). Unintended consequences of external testing in elementary schools. *Educational Measurement: Issues and Practice, 10*(4), 7–11.

Snipes, J., Doolittle, F., & Herlihy, C. (2002). *Foundations for success: Case studies of how urban school systems improve student achievement.* Washington, DC: Council of Great City Schools.

Solomon, R. (1992). *Black resistance in high school: Forging a separatist culture.* Albany, NY: SUNY Press.

Solomon, B., Booker, T., & Goldhaber, D. (2009, June). Boosting student achievement: The effect of comprehensive school reform on student achievement. *Educational Evaluation and Policy Analysis, 31*(2), 111–126.

Spring, J. (1991). Textbook writing and ideological management: A postmodern approach. In P. Altbach, G. Kelly, H. Petrie, & L. Weis (Eds.), *Textbooks in American Society* (pp. 185–200). Albany, NY: SUNY Press.

Squires, D. (2005). *Aligning and balancing the standards-based curriculum.* Thousand Oaks, CA: Corwin.

Svobodny, D. (Ed.) (1987). *Early American textbooks, 1775–1900: A catalog of the titles held by the Educaitonal Research Library.* Washington, DC: U.S. Department of Education.

Taba, H. (1962). *Curriculum development.* New York: Harcourt, Brace & World.

Tanner, D., & Tanner, L. (1990). *History of the school curriculum.* New York: Macmillan.

Taylor, C. (1999). To follow a rule . . . . In R. Shusterman (Ed.), *Bourdieu: A critical reader* (pp. 29–44). Oxford, UK: Blackwell Publishers.

Terman, L. M. (1916). *The measurement of intelligence.* Boston: Houghton Mifflin.

Thompson, J. (1967). *Organizations in action: Social science bases of administrative theory.* New York: McGraw-Hill.

Thompson, P. C. (1982). *Quality circles.* New York: American Management Association.

Tomsho, R. (2009, October 15). U.S. math scores hit a wall. *The Wall Street Journal,* A3.

Thorndike, E. L. (1913). *The psychology of learning: Vol. 2. Educational psychology.* New York: Teachers College, Bureau of Publications, Columbia University Press.

Tyack, D., & Hansot, E. (1990). *Learning together: A history of coeducation in American schools.* New York: The Russell Sage Foundation.

Tyler, R. (1974). The use of tests in measuring the effectiveness of educational programs, methods, and instructional materials. In R. W. Tyler & R. M. Wolf (Eds.), *Crucial issues in testing* (pp. 143–156). Berkeley, CA: McCutchan.

Tyler, R. W. (1949). *Basic principles of curriculum and instruction.* Chicago: University of Chicago Press.

Walder, A. (2009, September). Unruly stability: Why China's regime has staying power. *Current History, 108*(719), 257–263.

Venezky, R. (1992). Textbooks in school and society. In P. Jackson (Ed.), *Handbook of research on curriculum* (pp. 436–461). New York: Macmillan Publishing Company.

Viadero, D. (2009, October 14). Teacher compensation ripe for change authors say. *Education Week, 29*(7), 10.

Wallace, D. G. (1981). *Developing basic skills programs in secondary schools.* Alexandria, VA: Association of Supervision and Curriculum Development.

Webb, N. (1997, January). *Determining alignment of expectations and assessments in mathematics and science education.* (NIKSE Brief, Vol. 1 No. 2). Madison: University of Wisconsin, National Institute for Science Education.

Webb, N. (1999). *Alignment of science and mathematics standards and assessment in four states.* (NISE Research Monograph Number 18). Madison: National Institute for Science Education, University of Wisconsin-Madison: Washington, D.C. Council of Chief State School Officers.

Webb, N. (2002, April). *An analysis of the alignment between mathematics standards and assessment for three states.* Paper presented at the American Education Research Association, New Orleans, LA.

Weick, K. (1978, December). Educational organizations as loosely coupled systems. *Administrative Science Quarterly, 23,* 541–552.

Weinberg, N. (2003, October 6). Educating Eli. *Forbes,* 106–110.

West, C. (1999). Race and modernity. In C. West (Ed.) *The Cornell West Reader* (pp. 55–86). New York. Basic Civitas Books.

White, J. (2006). *Intelligence, destiny, and education.* Oxon, UK: Routeledge.

Whitehead, A. (1959). *The aims of education and other essays.* New York: The Macmillan Company.

Wolcott, H. F. (1977). *Teachers vs. technocrats.* Eugene, OR: Center for Policy and Management.

Woods, P. (2005). *Democratic leadership in education.* London, UK: Paul Chapman Publishing.

Yeh, S. (2001, May). Tests worth teaching to: Constructing state-mandated tests that emphasize critical thinking. *Educational Researcher, 30*(9), 12–17.

Yen, H. (2009, December 17). Census: White majority to end by midcentury. *The Atlanta Journal-Constitution*, A13.

Young, J. (2003, October 10). Researchers charge racial bias on the SAT. *The Chronicle of Higher Education, 40*(7), A34–A35.

Index

CORWIN
A SAGE Company

The Corwin logo—a raven striding across an open book—represents the union of courage and learning. Corwin is committed to improving education for all learners by publishing books and other professional development resources for those serving the field of PreK–12 education. By providing practical, hands-on materials, Corwin continues to carry out the promise of its motto: **"Helping Educators Do Their Work Better."**